Moments of Being

*...finding your
one moment in time*

NEW YORK

Moments of Being

...finding your one moment in time

by Barrie Brett

ISBN 978-160037-624-5 (paperback)
Library of Congress Control Number 2009924959

Published by:

MORGAN · JAMES
THE ENTREPRENEURIAL PUBLISHER™
www.morganjamespublishing.com

Morgan James Publishing, LLC
1225 Franklin Ave. Ste 325
Garden City, NY 11530-1693
Toll Free 800-485-4943
www.MorganJamesPublishing.com

Habitat for Humanity®
Peninsula
Building Partner

In an effort to support local communities, raise awareness and funds, Morgan James Publishing donates one percent of all book sales for the life of each book to Habitat for Humaity.

Get involved today, visit
www.HelpHabitatForHumanity.com

TABLE OF CONTENTS

Cecilia —
your children
are wonderful —
Hope your writing
finds success!
Wishing you
The best
of
moments!
Truly —
Barrie Brett

dedication

For Dana, Adam, Beth and darling Ilianna
For Mom, Dad and my "darlink" Grandma

Foreword

F. Murray Abraham

The high school teacher who invited me to try acting, something that was totally and completely foreign to me, is responsible for changing my life. And I don't have a clue why it happened.

The concept of the Big Break appears deceptively simple; when the opportunity of a lifetime presents itself we will naturally jump at the chance. It is not that simple at all, and is best illustrated by this parable of Moses and the burning bush. It seems that when God was finished with His instructions to Moses, he offered to answer one question of him. Moses asked, "Why did you choose this moment to show me the burning bush?" And God said, "It has always been burning."

The world is alive with opportunities of all kinds, mental, physical and moral. We do have choices, and in the end, our choices are who we are. If you're lucky enough to keep your eyes open and recognize these moments of choice, good things can happen. All things are possible.

This is exactly how I feel. Acting was always there, I just hadn't seen it before my high school teacher, Miss Hutchins, saw something in me and pointed me in that direction. I think we have to do whatever we can to see the bush. If we can open our eyes and not be afraid, a wonderful moment can be revealed. After all, the bush is always burning.

Moments of Being...
Finding Your One Moment in Time
Introduction

Moments of Being is a collection of true stories revealing life-altering experiences, personal challenges and triumphs. Not a day goes by that I don't hear about these "twist of fate" moments, from friends, family members and coworkers; in restaurants and at the movies; while reading newspapers and magazines; or during a chance meeting on an elevator or subway. I believe that if we pay attention to these moments, they can help shape who we are and who we might become.

It is my hope that you will read these stories and think about how you might have handled a similar moment, how *you* might recognize your own transforming moment, and as a result, see your life and perhaps your future change in an instant.

Moments of Being: My Journey

As a little girl in elementary school, I fell in love with the music of crooner Eddie Fisher, and then Steve Lawrence. When I was a teenager, I had a crush on entertainer Anthony Newley, and while everyone around me was cheering for major recording stars like Elvis, Frankie Avalon and Fabian, I was listening to Newley's show tunes. "Gonna Build a Mountain from a Little Hill," from the play *Stop the World—I Want to Get Off*, was one of my favorites. Though I don't have the prettiest singing voice (in fact, it's pretty bad), I sang the lyrics from this song continually.

As I grew older and my life struggles became greater, these words stayed with me. I didn't know exactly how I was "gonna do it," but

I was going to try to build my mountain from a little hill, just as the song said. I was going to try to recognize tiny moments as paths to big opportunities.

While I was going through my divorce, I was a stay at home mom with two young children. I had to take on three jobs to make ends meet. In order to have money for holiday gifts one year, I took a temporary sales job in the men's department of Bloomingdale's. It was here, during a casual coffee-break conversation, that a coworker mentioned a friend who had gotten a job on a new TV show in Washington, D.C.

As a former schoolteacher, there was nothing in my background to make me think I should or could apply to this new show. But I did. To this day, I still don't know why, but it turned out to be one of my best decisions ever. I started as an intern and was soon producing video pieces for what became a very popular nationally syndicated television show, *PM Magazine*. I was fortunate; the people I worked with were very talented and very generous with their knowledge and experience. My new career as a television producer was launched.

I went on to win Emmy Awards for producing and writing, and started my own production company in South Florida. Producing a variety of projects from commercials to features, magazine shows, documentaries, celebrity interviews, sports shows and corporate videos, I was very busy and successful. I was also working six to seven days a week, and my sleep was suffering. Not one to take medication, I decided to take a supplement from a health food store that guaranteed safe, uninterrupted sleep.

Unfortunately, that particular batch of L-Tryptophan was tainted. Many people died. I was fortunate: I survived. But it took its toll.

It took me two years to regain my health. Hospitalized, bedridden and misdiagnosed with a myriad of ailments ranging from paralysis to heart failure, I was beginning to think I would never get well and climb up that mountain again. But eventually, I did.

The two "moments" I mentioned were the start of an understanding; building my mountain from a little hill required listening to those moments. For me, the first moment was almost accidental: I heard about a new television show going on the air. If I hadn't taken my coffee break at that time, I probably would not have found out about that position. The second moment came when I ingested that tainted supplement. Both of these moments changed my life. The first led me in the direction of a new career, the second almost killed me. I not only had to fight hard to get my health back, but my astronomical medical bills combined with the fact that I couldn't work for two years forced me to use up all my savings and turn in my stocks and IRA account. I lost everything: my business, my house, even my car.

When I did regain my health, I built that mountain right up again, producing more and more, from talk shows and news specials to syndicated lifestyle programming. I moved back to the city I loved, New York, where I was born. And I began again.

Moments of Being: How It Began
Not long after I returned to New York, the idea for this book was inspired by three events that occurred in one week.

When I was working on a morning talk show, my mother sent me some information regarding her friend's son. He'd been a young professional golfer with a very promising career. One day, he met his friends for some recreational golf. While driving down an embankment, his golf cart tipped over, and he was thrown from the cart. At first, there didn't appear to be any apparent physical injuries, however, he was diagnosed as a paraplegic. He had to give up his dream of becoming a champion, but he was able to turn his accident into something positive. He now travels the country as a motivational speaker, and demonstrates how you can play golf while seated in the golf cart. I was moved by his story. Here was a young man with such promise who had dealt with incredible trauma, and he'd come back swinging. I knew I wanted to hear him tell his story.

That same week, I read an article about a woman who had been mugged. When the mugger took her purse and money, he started to cry. "I'm not really a thief," he said. "I lost my job and need money for my wife and children." He ended up giving back the purse. She ended up giving him the money. She said in the interview: "I wonder if that moment changed his life; it did mine."

That same week a third event happened. I was asked to attend a meeting with several people to see about developing some television projects. The dinner and discussion were stimulating, and I saw tremendous potential in working with this group. But then out of the blue, one of the participants began ranting about a newspaper article he read that week. He began raising his voice and banging on his plate with the silverware.

I sat watching him, and finally said, "What happened? We were having such a pleasant conversation. Why did you get so upset about the news article?"

He said, "One day I was a perfectly average, controlled individual. Then I read about the injustice of certain laws, and in one moment I became a raving lunatic. I can't help myself; I just get so upset whenever I hear about them!" His answer confirmed what I was already thinking: I had to put together a collection of "moment in time" stories.

I went home that evening and wrote my first proposal for a book entitled *One Moment in Time*.

After that, I became fascinated with finding other such stories, and I wanted to see whether there was a pattern or reason for these "moments in time." I was reminded of the song I used to sing over and over again. Sometimes just being aware of these moments can help you climb up that hill and change your life forever.

Moments of Being Finds Its Voice

When I was young, the book that most affected my life was *The Bridge of San Luis Rey* by Thornton Wilder. I remember reading it over and over again. I asked myself: Why were the main characters on the same bridge at the same time when it collapsed? Why did they all fall to their deaths? Who were these people, and why were they there at that one moment in time?

When I became a television producer, I was fascinated by the "back story." When I interviewed my story subjects—whether celebrities, business leaders, everyday workers, men or women—I was curious: what was that *something* in their backgrounds that brought them to this point in their lives?

When I started researching and gathering stories for this book, I focused on each person's transforming moment. What was it about these people that made them realize that their lives were changed in just that—a moment? I began to see a similar thread woven into each story.

Each person developed an *awareness*, made an *acknowledgment*, or took *action* when their moment came. I began to think of this in terms of "A-A-A." For each of the people I interviewed, there was an *awareness* that something happened to bring about change. Each of them had *acknowledged* that change was possible. And each of them took some kind of *action* to produce the change.

I also thought back to my own moments. When my colleague told me about his friend's new job, I had *awareness*. I *acknowledged* the fact that I wanted to better my life and my situation. And I took *action*: I called for an interview.

When I was busy producing and wasn't sleeping well, I took the tainted supplement from the health food store, and there was an awareness that something had happened. There was an acknowledgment that I was sick. And there was action taken in striving to get better and later in moving back to New York to re-start my career.

There are instances when not all of the "A's" occur at the same moment. Sometimes *awareness* comes years later. Sometimes *acknowledgment* and *action* are delayed as well, but in almost every story in this book, lives were definitively changed in just one moment.

When you read these stories, I hope you will consider your own feelings about each moment, and how you would have reacted if faced with a similar situation. What would *you* do in that moment? In this book, I've included an interactive component so that you can put yourself in the story and assess how you might have handled each moment. I'm also including a "Map Your Moment" chart for you to practice recognizing your own past and potential *Moments of Being*.

Moments of Being: The Stars
This book has been in the works for almost fifteen years. As a busy television producer, my projects took me away from writing for extended periods of time, but throughout the years, I continued to meet new and interesting people and collect stories of change. I'm so

grateful to each and every one of the amazing men and women who agreed to be interviewed by me and share their *Moments of Being*.

As an interviewer, I've had the privilege of meeting with celebrities, as well as men and women from across the country and from a variety of professions and circumstances. I love the process of researching story subjects and learning about their lives. I met in person with the people in this book whenever possible, or else conducted phone interviews with them. I have endeavored to keep each story true to the interview and to present each person's story in his or her own voice. Two people asked that their full names not be used, and I honored that request. I am very grateful for everyone's willingness to share personal thoughts and transformations with me—and now with you, the reader. I hope you find their stories as moving as I have.

Moments of Being: The Title and Virginia Woolf

Almost a decade ago, I had a conversation with my friend, Ron. He asked me about my book project and shared an experience he had as a young boy, one that he felt totally changed the way he looked at life. Just before conducting my final interview for this book, I suddenly remembered our conversation and set up a meeting to interview him. Ron described that childhood experience as his "moment of being."

Coincidentally, around the same time, an acquaintance had suggested that I read Virginia Woolf's *Moments of Being, A Collection of Autobiographical Writing*. During each of the interviews that shaped this book, there was a moment when I actually felt the proverbial goose bumps on my arms; I knew when that happened that I was hearing each person's moment of transformation. While reading Virginia Woolf's words, I got those goose bumps all over again. It wasn't so much a particular quote that affected me, but rather a series of thoughts she expressed about receiving "sudden shocks" or "moments of being."

> *"...Though I still have the peculiarity that I receive these sudden shocks, they are now always welcome; after the first surprise, I always feel instantly that they are particularly valuable..."*[1]

For almost fifteen years, my title for this book project had been *One Moment in Time*; I had also considered *Twist of Fate, Serendipity,* and *Magic Moments*. But after hearing about Ron's experience combined with reading Virginia Woolf, there was no question in my mind: my title had to be *Moments of Being...Finding Your One Moment in Time*.

Moments of Being: Finding Your One Moment in Time

My deepest wish is that the stories in this book can, in some small way, help shape who you are and who you might become. There are those who may become *aware* and *acknowledge* their moment (or multiple moments), and who may, depending upon the *action* they take, see their lives change in miraculous ways. For others, this process may take some time. But whichever category you fall into, remember that the process is your own.

I'm fond of the lyrics from *Seasons of Love* in the Broadway show, *Rent*: There are *"525,000 moments so dear."*[2] You never know when one of those moments could become your *Moment of Being*!

I hope you will share your reactions and your own stories with me!

Fondly,

Barrie Brett

1.

Teachers Do Make A Difference

Years ago, I taught second grade cultural arts and writing. I consider teaching to be a noble profession and value the dedication of those who stay on this path. That's why I've chosen to start this book with teacher-inspired moments.

I was thrilled that the following two immensely talented men agreed to share their memories and *moments* here. As you'll see, both of their lives were transformed by a devoted teacher.

"I believe things that happen to change our lives are legitimate openings, and are revealed to offer opportunities."

- F. Murray Abraham

F. Murray Abraham is a highly regarded stage and screen actor. He has received both the Academy and Golden Globe Awards for his brilliant performance as Salieri in *Amadeus*, and his distinguished resume includes performances in classical and contemporary plays. As an avid admirer of his work, I've seen most of his films, television shows and stage performances, and think he's one of our finest actors.

Murray's early years were far removed from the worlds of film and theater. In fact he might never have entered the acting world at all, if not for one teacher, and one moment that transformed him from a rebellious youth into a dedicated actor.

A Teacher's Gift

F. Murray Abraham's Story

A child of hard-working, blue-collar immigrant parents from Italy and Syria, I grew up in El Paso, Texas. My dad was a mechanic, and many members of my family were steel and coal workers. Around my home, most of the days were filled with work and more work, and there was little time for entertainment.

At the age of twelve, I was diagnosed with rheumatic fever, and became quite ill. I spent much of the next year in bed. During this time I became interested in books and reading; although I had never read much before, now I had little else to do. And so I read, hour after hour, day after day. I fell in love with books and words.

When I emerged from this experience, I exploded into a tumultuous adolescence. I started getting into trouble and acting wild with neighborhood friends. This phase could have gone on to become truly destructive if not for one of my high school teachers, Lucia P. Hutchins.

Before becoming a teacher, Miss Hutchins had gone to New York to try her hand at acting. Unfortunately, she had not received much acclaim. A stocky woman, she had a flair for dressing in distinct, bright colors that made you take notice of her. She, in turn, noticed me.

Now almost seventeen years old, I had little interest in the theater and no knowledge of acting. But Miss Hutchins saw something in me. She suggested I try a drama and speech class, and for my first attempt at performance start with a one-act play by J.M. Barrie, *The Old Lady Shows Her Medals.*

From that first day of drama class, I changed my ways. I stopped hanging around with my neighborhood friends and started working on my acting abilities. I read extensively and listened to recordings of great actors such as John Gielgud and John Barrymore. I also recorded my own voice and listened to myself. I discovered that I didn't like what I heard, so I worked on my diction. I didn't think my Texas-Mexico border accent would survive in the acting world.

I think it was because Miss Hutchins believed in me that I listened to her. I'm glad I did. That first performance led to my joining a drama team and participating in a local competition, which we won. This led to a state competition, which we also won, and that helped me receive a college scholarship to the University of Texas, El Paso, where I studied acting. After graduation, I practiced my craft in Los Angeles and then in New York, studying with actress and legendary teacher Uta Hagen.

From the moment I stepped into that first drama class, I knew that's where I belonged. I can't explain it, but I knew my life was changed forever. Until then, I thought that I'd spend my life working at some low-paying job, that I'd probably get drunk a lot, that I'd never find any real direction. In the play *Gypsy*, Gypsy Rose sings, "Got the dream but not the guts."[3] I believe you can discover your calling, but then you have to have the guts to give it a shot. When you run into someone who has faith in you, you owe it to him or her to go for it. Miss Hutchins, God rest her soul, saw something in me that opened my future.

I'm now fortunate to have the opportunity to perform all around the world, on stage and on film. I'm also a drama teacher in New York

City and strongly believe in the importance of offering opportunities to others. I take the responsibility of "seeing something" in my students quite seriously. When I'm acting in films and plays around the world, I like to offer classes for young actors: it's a way to give back, and I believe I get something back from them as well. The acting world is a community, and the interaction between teacher and student helps create that sense of community.

I believe things that happen to change our lives are legitimate openings and are revealed to offer opportunities. We just have to keep our eyes open to recognize these moments. I feel I've been fortunate to recognize all the opportunities offered to me, and it all started because of a single moment with Lucia P. Hutchins.

Moments of Being A-A-A

Awareness—Acknowledgment—Action

Here's an opportunity for you to start the process of *mapping your moment* using the stories in each chapter of this book. After reading each story, there will be a box (like the one on the oppposite page) where you can record the moment of *awareness* and/or *acknowledgment* and the *action* taken. Would you have reacted the same way as the person in the story? If not, you can write the action you would have taken instead. Do you think the outcome would have been the same?

This interactive exercise gives you the opportunity to practice recognizing *moments*, so that hopefully you will be able to acknowledge your own *moments* when they appear. At the end of the book, there will be a section where you can map your own *Moments of Being*.

Following is the first A-A-A for F. Murray Abraham's Story.

A-A-A: Map the Moment

What was the moment of *Awareness*?

_____

_____

_____

What was the moment of *Acknowledgment*?

_____

_____

_____

What was the *Action* taken?

_____

_____

_____

"I couldn't read as quickly as my classmates… To compensate, I became the class clown, the great distracter."

- Morry Alter

For over two decades, Morry Alter reported the news with the number one television market in the country: WCBS-TV in New York City. His news pieces stand out for their humor and human interest value. With at least twenty-two Emmy Awards to his credit, Morry is well-known for his distinctive writing skills and quirky sense of humor. He's a natural whether reporting live or on taped pieces, and his written and verbal communication skills are hard to beat. On TV, a report from him is often called "A Morry Story."

I was pleased to be his producer more than twenty-five years ago in Miami, Florida, where he hosted a weekly magazine show; we have remained friends ever since. When he told me that he didn't always have a way with words, I knew I had to hear his story.

Here's the moment behind every "Morry Story," a wake-up call that literally came as one swift blow.

Young Man, You Can Write!
Morry Alter's Story

As a young boy in Davenport, Iowa, I had trouble in school. Though not officially diagnosed, it was thought that I had a learning disability in reading, which made school very difficult for me. I was a terrible student. I was painfully slow in class and probably would have been held back a grade or two if it hadn't been for the respect my parents received in the community. Reading was a struggle and this carried over into all subjects.

At about eleven years old, I remember pretending to read. When a fellow student gave a report and held up a cartoon with a bubble caption and the whole class laughed, I pretended to understand the joke, even though I couldn't read as quickly as my classmates and had no idea what was so funny. To compensate, I became the class clown, the great distracter.

During my sophomore year in high school, in a desperate attempt to "straighten me out," my parents enrolled me in a private Catholic school. I was the only Jewish student enrolled there. Though discipline was sometimes harsh, only one priest ever slapped me. I think there was a spoken or unspoken consensus to "lay off the kid from Temple Emanuel."

We were in glee club one day, and there I was, the great distracter, flying a paper airplane, when the smack came. It shocked me, but something about Father Boyle's decision to subject me to equal justice impressed me as well.

Father Boyle was also my English teacher. One day, he assigned us to write a short story with a science fiction theme. When he handed back the story, I expected to see the usual comment of "This won't do," or "This is no good." But instead, he had written, *"Young man, you can write!"* And if that wasn't enough, he had my little story published in the St. Ambrose College newspaper, with a byline! Pretty heady stuff for a kid who'd have been happy with a "C" instead of the "A" that was emblazoned on my short story!

I knew that my teacher was a member of the highly educated Jesuit order, and had been educated in Rome: in short, any praise from this guy was a serious compliment. His encouragement lit my fire and gave me the confidence to write creatively. The more I wrote, the more I enjoyed it.

For some reason I had always liked reading out loud, perhaps because that kind of reading was literally more my speed. Now, just for the fun of it, I'd spend time reading aloud what I wrote. Who knew? But what I do know is that Father Boyle's rave review sparked a major turnaround in my life.

Around that time, my parents re-enrolled me in public school. I may have been back at my old stomping grounds, but I was a different student now. Father Boyle's words had been an educational jumpstart. At Bettendorf High School, I started doing well on essay tests and joined the speech team. I won statewide awards for interpretive reading of my own writing, and the writing of others. For the first time in my school career, I was the best at something.

Gradually I started to read more and more, even if it wasn't a lot faster. Along the way, I discovered Ernest Hemingway. He was so easy to read! Short, declarative sentences. He wrote the way people talked. I never got as good as Hemingway, but he showed me the way: his use of language was perfect for the competitions, and helped me succeed in my interpretive readings. So here's to Father Boyle, Papa Hemingway and *The Old Man and the Sea*!

I went on to college, a place one guidance counselor thought I'd never be. But there I was, keeping an eye out for courses that included essay tests! After graduating from the State University of Iowa with a political science major, being perhaps less than directed, I held various jobs, including one as a probation officer. Two years later I was back at the university, working on a graduate degree in public relations.

Over that summer, I worked at a radio station in Davenport, Iowa. There, I got a job on air, almost by accident. One night, after the newsman got in trouble for writing bad checks, I volunteered to do the news without pay. The station owner wasn't going to pass up a deal like that. I not only read, but wrote the stories!

That summer news job convinced me to change my Master's course of study from Public Relations to Radio/TV news. And that was it. For forty years now, "it"—read'n and write'n—has been pretty darned rewarding. Along the way, I was even asked to teach the writing part of my job at Northwestern's Medill School of Journalism.

As I take stock of things, I give all the credit to the writing. Not mine—to Father Boyle's five little words on that 10th grade paper: *"Young man, you can write."*

A-A-A: Map the Moment

What was the moment of *Awareness*?

_____

_____

_____

_____

What was the moment of *Acknowledgment*?

_____

_____

_____

_____

What was the *Action* taken?

_____

_____

_____

_____

2.

One Quest... One Telegram... One Report

There are decisions we make in just ONE moment that alter the rest of our lives. For the following three men, that's exactly what happened. As a result, a lifelong vision was realized, a family was born, and a life was saved and reshaped.

"Impossible is only in your mind."

- Gary Hirshberg

Psychologist Dr. Debi Warner told me of an exciting seminar she attended, which she found to be helpful and encouraging to entrepreneurs and business owners. She knew of my book project and suggested I speak to Gary Hirshberg, the sponsor of the Stonyfield Farm Entrepreneurship Institute.

If you're a yogurt eater, you know the name Stonyfield Farm. This organic yogurt brand is a leader in its field, and Gary Hirshberg is this company's leader and "CE-Yo." Gary's entry into the field of yogurt production came as the result of what he calls an epiphany. That moment, along with a few others, started him on a personal quest and eventually gave him the means to help others with their life choices.

The Man From Stonyfield
Gary Hirshberg's Story

I grew up in New Hampshire, the eldest of five children. My father was a successful businessman, my mother a homemaker.

My parents divorced when I was fourteen years old. Soon after the divorce, my father's business started to fail and my mom became the sole supporter of our family, working for a friend in the hotel industry. She worked hard and rose to become senior buyer for the Sheraton Hotel chain. From there, she transferred to Disney and became the senior buyer for the EPCOT project; it was her job to find and purchase everything from carpeting to plumbing supplies. One year, she asked me to help her find a birch bark canoe! If you've been to EPCOT Center at Disneyworld in Florida, you know how huge the area is, and my mother helped fill it with product. She was an amazing role model for us.

I had two contrasting models as I watched the decline of my dad's business compared to my mother's rising career. She'd done the impossible, rising from nothing to the top of her field in record time. Watching my mother's growth, I developed an understanding that "impossible is only in your mind." This idea would become very meaningful in my life.

Growing up, the mountains of New Hampshire were my backyard. I was a skier and a racer, and I was passionate about the outdoors. As time passed, I watched the farms around my hometown start to disappear. Mountaintop views changed as the open spaces previously occupied by farms faded, swept away by an ebbing tide of farm profitability and a changing view of land use. The open fields, barns and chicken coops of my childhood were replaced by housing developments and industrial parks. I was very affected by this. When it was time for me to go to college I chose to study climate and environmental changes. After graduation, I decided to continue on that path in grad school.

It was at this time that I had an epiphany: I realized that the science elite were identifying the problems of climate change, but were not developing programs focused on solutions. In the late 1970s, I decided it was my task to focus on those solutions. I left my graduate studies and began work on wind engineering and organic agriculture at The Alchemy Institute in Cape Cod. There, I studied organic farming methods, and learned how to build windmills. The teaching here was very advanced in the areas of food storage at commercial levels, and energy production that left no "carbon footprint." The Institute was very much ahead of its time, and only now are the ideas that were taught there being appreciated.

I eventually became the executive director of The Alchemy Institute, and it was my task to find our funding, over a million dollars a year. It was now the early 1980s, and funding was being slashed for renewable energy research and development. One evening, I was scheduled as the keynote speaker for the National Solar Energy Commission. That very night, a tax cut for renewable energy funding was announced, affecting everyone in the audience. It was like speaking to a group of ghosts.

Right after my speech, I boarded an airplane to Florida for a scheduled visit with my mother. While walking around EPCOT the next day, I passed the Kraft Foods Big Land Pavilion, which featured an impressive display showing how humans evolved from being hunter/gatherers to using techniques of modern agriculture. The exhibit focused on modern technology, heralding the future of food production.

I was immediately engaged. The contrast was so apparent to me. At the Alchemy Institute, we were teaching people how they could eat three meals a day, 365 days a year, using no fossil fuels, chemicals or pesticides—while the Kraft Pavilion was exhibiting traditional methods of food production which I believed would harm the environment by burning fossil fuel. Here was this beautiful pavilion being heated with oil in sunny Central Florida, where solar energy would be an obvious alternate energy source, and promoting a "big business" approach to food production which used large amounts of pesticides and herbicides.

I asked the tour guide how many people came to view this building. The answer astounded me and changed my career direction. He said, "Twenty-five thousand people a day come through here."

When I heard those words, standing there in front of the Kraft Pavilion, I was truly taken aback. And I had an epiphany.

At our institute, we had twenty-five thousand visitors a year who came to learn about food production with ecology as a focus, but *twenty-five thousand people a day* came through this part of EPCOT! I decided at that moment that I had to become Kraft Foods. I had to get the power of big business behind me, so that I could teach that many people about another method of food production: namely, organic agriculture.

I told my mother that I had to go into business. She was shocked: remember, I'd seen my dad's successful business fail, and I'd always said that big business was not for me. In fact, I hated business! But after the recent reductions in major funding for alternative energy sources, I realized that I needed the power of business to get my environmental message across. I wanted to start something that would get people to move into my space, and create a place that would help people understand the importance of organic foods and their means of production.

So why yogurt?

As executive director of The Alchemy Institute, I was also a trustee of the school for organic farming. The director of this center, Samuel (who has since become my business partner), had seven cows and a delicious yogurt recipe that he would serve at our board meetings. The announced lack of grant funding for energy had taken away backing that the school needed to continue. Struggling to meet financial obligations, we decided to start selling the yogurt to make up for lost funding. In 1983, we borrowed $35,000 and started producing yogurt.

From that moment in EPCOT when the tour guide told me how many people visited there every day, I knew I had to do things differently and change my methods of operation if I wanted to reach people with my message about organic farming. Now, we were starting that process. The problem, of course, was that neither Samuel nor I knew a thing about running a business. But we did have a great recipe!

We raised more funds with the help of family and friends, and we grew day by day. We made mistake after mistake along the way, but somehow by 1987 we had outgrown the capacity of Stonyfield, our little hilltop farm in New Hampshire, and we decided to buy a dairy.

We had a friend in Massachusetts who ran a dairy without a branded product. Since we had a product without a dairy, we thought it would be a good business marriage—but it was not. We were naïve, and we didn't do all the financial background checks we should have done. Although we tried for many months to make it work, traveling back and forth between New Hampshire and Massachusetts, our friend came up against a personal Chapter 7 bankruptcy, and we were forced to bring our production back to Stonyfield Farm in New Hampshire.

Our biggest problem was that we had tripled our sales after moving to Massachusetts, and our volume was now too large to produce on our little farm. There was no way we could keep up with the demand, and we were losing $20,000 each week. We didn't have the financial security to be in that position. We tried to meet our financial obligations by asking family and friends for support. Samuel and I would alternate, staying awake every other night to make the yogurt, desperately trying to keep up with demand.

Then, opportunity knocked—or so we thought. We entered into negotiations with a big dairy in Vermont, who would invest in our business and allow us to make our yogurt at their plant. Samuel and I had an incredible amount of debt, my wife was one month away from delivering our first child, and without a doubt we were eager to get this deal done. Still, we spent two months negotiating. We wanted to make sure that the people who had helped us (our shareholders now) were taken care of properly.

At last, we drove up to Vermont to get the deal signed. But when we arrived, it was clear the deal was not going to happen. The people across the table presented us with completely different terms than we'd agreed to, a deal which basically amounted to stealing our company. We got up from the table and walked out.

Needless to say, the ride home was quite different from the ride up to that meeting. Our earlier eagerness had turned to despair. Besides the negative outcome of the meeting, we were now driving in a major snowstorm. In fact, it was a blizzard. Though it had taken us only two hours to drive up to the dairy, it was taking three times as long to get back, and our day wasn't nearly over, since we had yogurt to make that very night. All we could think about was the reality of our situation. It seemed clear to us that we had no future!

At one point during that drive, we decided there was no use crying over spilled milk—or in our case, spilled yogurt. I asked Samuel, "If money were not a problem, what do you think would be the minimum amount needed to build our own yogurt plant?"

As Samuel drove, I flipped on the dome light in the car and we started making notes. It seemed a little crazy: I was going home to face my very pregnant wife to whom I had promised a signed deal when I returned, Samuel and I had an all-nighter of yogurt-making ahead of us, and now we were designing our own plant?

When we finally got home, my wife asked if the deal was done. I said, "We have a better idea."

Somehow, it worked. We were able to put a deal together with a bank's support, and we opened our plant eight months later. A year later, we made a profit. Ten years after launching Stonyfield, we surpassed Kraft Foods in yogurt sales. Our goal had been reached. We were getting our message of environmental consciousness out to the public. We were producing organic yogurt on a large scale using fresh ingredients, a terrific recipe and a lot of TLC, and we were still tending to each production like it was a fine wine. Not only did I become like Kraft, but in a way Kraft became a little like me: recently they introduced their first organic sliced American cheese singles.

I'm not sure I understand it all, but the epiphanies I have experienced seem to have something in common. Changing my grad studies, visiting EPCOT and hearing the number of people who visited the

Kraft Pavilion each day, sitting in the middle of a blizzard with Samuel designing our yogurt plant and planning the future of our business—every one of these moments involved making a decision.

There's a moment when you go to that place inside you—a reserve, or insanity, or maybe a well of belief in oneself—and that moment leads you to both a decision and the ability to act on that decision. It was that moment and that place that Samuel and I drew from, and found a way to begin again. I learned at a young age that "impossible is only in your mind." There is always an answer, as long as you don't quit. Determination is an undervalued attribute, and one of the primary ingredients for success. At that moment in the car, Samuel and I were able to dig deep and find a solution that we never could have imagined just hours before. We regrouped.

Samuel and I learned a lot about business over the years. We now have an Institute for Entrepreneurs at Stonyfield, and each year scores of businesspeople gather to share growing pains and solutions. We offer information and problem solving skills I wish I had known when we were growing our business. Every mistake we could have made in those early years, we made, but now we can share our experiences with others through this forum.

When I think about "moments," I think the only thing that exists is the present. We could be kinder and more successful as a species, and as a planet, if we could live in the present and not put off things for later. I believe when you grab your moment, you unleash incredible potential. I'm incredibly grateful that I recognized my moments, and I hope others have a similar chance to recognize their own.

A-A-A: Map the Moment

What was the moment of *Awareness*?

_____

_____

_____

_____

What was the moment of *Acknowledgment*?

_____

_____

_____

_____

What was the *Action* taken?

_____

_____

_____

_____

"I believe the next moment may be the one that sets up the rest of your life. All of us are like plants that flower at different times: how we water our flowers, and the circumstance of each moment, determines our life's direction."

- Steven R.

In 1968, passions were running high. That year, we witnessed escalating violence in Vietnam and the assassination of national leaders. Student protests were staged across the nation. Tensions were building, and young people were looking for a way to make a difference.

That year, scores of young people applied to serve in the Peace Corps, each with their own dream of bridging the barriers of culture and strife in the name of a greater good. One of them was Steven R. Little did Steven know that a single telegram would change not only his own future but the future of two families.

I've known Steven for decades. He's my brother's good friend, so he wasn't surprised when I called to interview him for this book. I knew a little of his story; still, hearing the details of his coincidental moment, I was amazed. Some things are just meant to be!

A Peace Corps Moment

Steven R.'s Story

In 1968, I was a recent college graduate faced with a very adult decision: I had applied for two positions, and now I had to make a choice between them.

This was not a choice between two office positions, or two sales jobs. No, this was a choice which, when made, would set me on one of two extremely different paths. And so I spent weeks going back and forth in indecision: should I attend graduate school at Harvard University, or should I join the Peace Corps? On the one hand, I felt that I had a calling to help others, but my family really wanted me to continue my education, and an opportunity to study at Harvard wasn't something to be taken lightly.

Eventually, I followed my heart. I chose the Peace Corps.

My destination would be Bogotá, Colombia. I was so excited that I started packing a week in advance. As the time of my departure neared, my duffle bag was almost full; there was only room for one final item. I decided that item should be a ham radio, something my friends had advised me to bring along on this journey so I would be able to stay connected to the outside world. (After all, this was way before e-mail or cell phones!)

I had just returned from buying the radio when my doorbell rang. I opened the door, and there stood a messenger holding a telegram from the Peace Corps office. The telegram said I was being rejected from the Peace Corps because of my bad knees, the result of a fencing injury in high school.

I was devastated. My packing was almost finished, and I had just bought that new radio from Abercrombie & Fitch. I was ready to go! All those long nights of agonizing over this decision, only to be rejected at the last moment!

In the end, of course, I unpacked my duffel bag, put my ham radio on a shelf and accepted the graduate position at Harvard. On my first day in the program, I met a fellow architectural student named Rebecca. Thirty years later, we're happily married with two grown children. Had I gone into the Peace Corps as I planned, I would never have met this wonderful woman and built a life and a family with her.

But that's not the end of the story.

Twenty-seven years after my experience with the Peace Corps, I was invited to sit on an all-day architectural panel and struck up a conversation with another architect seated next to me. Though we'd never met, Richard and I lived and worked within an hour's drive of each other. Somehow, over the course of the day, our conversation turned to the Peace Corps. We realized that we had both been assigned to begin training in Escondido, CA at the same time, August of 1968. The more we talked, the more we began to realize our connection.

Because I received that telegram, I was not able to go on my assignment to Bogotá; instead, I went to graduate school and met my wife. At the same time, Richard, who had been assigned to a different location, petitioned the Peace Corps for a change of assignment. It seems that just before training, he had met the love of his life, and the two of them wanted to marry and start out life together on their

Peace Corps missions. But there was a problem: Connie was assigned to Bogotá, and he was not. At first, his request to transfer to Bogotá was denied, but due to my last-minute rejection, a spot opened up and Richard was able to join the woman who became his wife.

In the span of one moment in 1968—the moment in which I read that telegram—four lives were altered forever.

A-A-A: Map the Moment

What was the moment of *Awareness*?

_____

_____

_____

_____

What was the moment of *Acknowledgment*?

_____

_____

_____

_____

What was the *Action* taken?

_____

_____

_____

_____

Moments of Being *...finding your one moment in time*

"When I put my mind to something, I can get the job done."

- Al Arden

These words have motivated Al Arden for most of his sixty-eight years. As a teenager, he triumphed on the ice rink, winning championships in skating and hockey. With the help of his wife Helen, a former high–fashion model, he built a highly successful clothing business catering to an upscale clientele; then, he changed direction and launched the company into the powerful hip-hop/urban market.

When I was thinking about getting my real estate license, my brother's friend, Steven, suggested that I speak to Helen Arden, who at that time was working as a real estate agent. He felt that Helen would offer keen advice since she was a seasoned agent and had helped members of his family find and sell apartments. Helen was just lovely and very supportive. Speaking with her, I mentioned my book project. She told me about her husband Al, whose lifelong ability to focus his mind on a goal hadn't only helped him build his career—it helped him change his life and turn weight loss into gold!

Goodbye Weight, Hello Gold
Al Arden's Story

When I was fifty-six years old, I went to the doctor for a routine checkup.

At the time, I was consumed by work. I never worked out; I just worked hard. I weighed in at two hundred and fifteen pounds, and had a 38-inch waist. I often had trouble breathing, and I'd been experiencing back pain for years. Despite these red flags, I never gave any thought to the fact that I was out of shape, but at my doctor's suggestion I agreed to get my heart checked.

The doctor put me on a treadmill. After six minutes, I was huffing and puffing, and the doctor hauled me off to check my blood pressure. It was 220 over 130. I couldn't believe my body was that out of whack.

My doctor brought me into his office, and said to me, "Do you want to die tomorrow? Because if you don't do something now, you're a prime candidate for a heart attack. You're someone who could be found dead on the street any minute."

Those words, heard at that moment, changed my life forever. I didn't want to die. But if I wanted to live I had to get my health back, and I had to be honest with myself. The last time I'd gotten any legitimate exercise was as a kid on the ice rink.

After additional coronary tests, a fifty percent heart blockage was found, and it became even more important for me to get moving immediately. But how would I go about it?

The first thing I did was start walking. At first, I couldn't walk ten New York City blocks before I turned around and staggered home in exhaustion. But I forced myself to keep at it, and soon I was walking twelve or fifteen blocks at a stretch. Not long after that, I was able to increase my walks to two miles.

When I reached the two mile mark, I made what was a major decision for me: I joined a gym. Applying the same mindset which had seen me through to success as a skater and a clothing designer, I threw myself into physical fitness. I started lifting weights and eating right. Muscle started replacing flab. Little by little, I watched my body change. By working out consistently and following a high-protein diet, I lost forty-five pounds over the next year. I no longer had a breathing problem. My back pain disappeared.

Once I began to see results from my efforts, I started working out seven days a week. From early morning to late afternoon, I focused on my fitness, lifting weights instead of packing weight on. Today, ten years later, people tell me I have a 'body of steel' and that I look like a much younger man. I'm six feet tall, weigh 173 pounds, and have a 32-inch waist. But most importantly, I have no lingering heart problems.

Walking started it all for me, and I've kept doing it through the years. My walks are now five miles long. To keep them interesting, I've made a game out of walking the streets of New York City. This started when I began picking up the coins I found lying in the street. At first, I would pick up a penny here and there. That turned into more pennies, dimes, quarters, even dollar bills. Now that I was looking, I discovered coins that hadn't dropped completely into parking meter slots. I also started a collection of discarded subway metro cards, which have hundreds of dollars of value still on them.

Finding money in the streets enhanced my walking routine. It felt like being rewarded for my efforts. The more money I found, the more I wanted to keep walking to search for more. Finding one dollar could keep me going for several miles. And these discoveries added up: some years, my finds totaled several thousand dollars. Walking had become a game, and it was fun.

Ten years ago, I was overweight, unhealthy, and in pain. Three years ago, I looked at myself to find that my whole body had changed. I was slim, muscular, and toned. My heart was healthy again, and my back didn't hurt. I felt wonderful, and I still do.

Many people need a wake-up call. I got mine the moment the doctor told me I could die tomorrow. Since then, I've changed my body and my life. I've even started writing a book to encourage anyone at any age to start getting fit, because it's never too late. I did it, and so can they!

A-A-A: Map the Moment

What was the moment of *Awareness*?

_____

_____

_____

_____

What was the moment of *Acknowledgment*?

_____

_____

_____

_____

What was the *Action* taken?

_____

_____

_____

_____

3.

The Gift of Life

Two women, one incredible bond.

"Moments do change lives. If you recognize and are open to your moment, your life will be enriched."

- Pam Garrett

Years ago, I produced a television piece with entertainer/pianist Ira Shore. He had developed a way of teaching called "How to Play Piano in Five Easy Steps." I later helped him with a video that explained his unique method; during this time, I became friends with Ira and his wife Rita. Our friendship grew as his talented family, The Singing Shores, performed at various functions I helped organize.

One day, when I was telling Ira about my project, he said, "You might want to speak with my daughter Steffi's life partner, Pam Garrett. She has a special moment you'll want to hear." Taking his advice, I interviewed both Steffi and Pam, and discovered an incredible moment and a selfless gift.

The Gift of Life
Pam Garrett's Story

Soon after starting a new job with a land development company, I was diagnosed with glaucoma.

Three years prior to the diagnosis, I'd started experiencing headaches that felt like a hot poker between my eyes. I went to see a neurologist, who diagnosed stress and told me that I needed a psychiatrist. The pain grew so intense that the psychiatrist prescribed morphine to treat it, along with high doses of other strong prescriptions.

After three years, I'd had enough. Not only were the pain medications—which by then included over 2,000 mg of opiates a day—making me feel dreadful, they weren't helping my headaches. I felt truly desperate. One day while stopped at a red light, I said a prayer to God. "I can't live like this," I said. "I don't know what's wrong with me. Please, I need your help!"

The next day, I thought I had an infection from my contact lens and decided to pick up some drops from an eye doctor whose office was close to my workplace. In fact, the office was directly across the street from the stoplight where I'd said my prayer. As the doctor examined me, I described my headache symptoms, and he said, "This is the worst case of glaucoma I've ever seen."

He told me that the next stage in the progression of the disease would have been blindness. He immediately performed laser surgery, and followed up with a few more surgeries. This doctor was my angel:

not only did he save my eyesight; he took me off the pain medications that were making me sick.

I was so thankful that my glaucoma was diagnosed in time. I'd always dreamed of working with my hands, and if I'd gone blind my dreams would have been shattered. When I started to feel better, I realized that it was time to act, and I enrolled in massage school. I'd been in constant pain for several years, and now I wanted to help others manage their own pain.

After graduating from massage school, I opened a practice working with a rheumatologist. It was a good partnership: this doctor believed that 80% of pain was muscular, and that massage helped to stretch the muscle and therefore decrease the pain. But after eight years there, I realized I had to earn more and took a higher-paying job in a mortgage office.

I can say honestly that I despised this job from the start. I knew it wasn't what I was meant to be doing, but I was determined to bring in some extra money, and I stayed with it for about a year while still working with my private clients.

Then, something happened that changed everything.

My life partner, Stephanie, is a cantor at a Temple in South Florida. One of her congregants sent out an e-mail, which Steph forwarded to me. It read:

Our son, Mason Steinmark, is seriously ill and is suffering from kidney failure. Mason is on a national transplant list, but he has been told that his wait can take up to another two years before he receives a cadaver's kidney. His physical, mental and emotional conditions are very bleak. His daily existence consists of being attached to a dialysis machine for a total of fourteen hours each day and self-injecting medicines. His life in the last two years has been severely limited. We do not know if he will survive the wait.

We are asking for someone to donate a kidney. The donor should have type O blood and should not suffer from hypertension (high blood pressure). Everyone can live on one kidney. As a matter of fact, just one kidney does the bulk of the work; the other kidney is more of a back up. The surgery will take place at Jackson Memorial Hospital in Miami. If done laparoscopically, the donor will probably be in the hospital for three to four days, and will be able to resume all activities in two weeks. Blood type testing, CT scan, medical examination and psychological testing are required of the donor. No costs are incurred by the donor. Our insurance will cover everything.

Thank you for your help.
Fran and Fred Steinmark

It was a plea from a desperate mom with a very sick son. Mason was thirty-two years old. His emotional and physical state was miserable; he was just existing. It was no life, being attached to a machine fourteen hours a day. His mother could not donate her kidney due to a heart valve problem, and neither his father, his brother nor his sister was a match.

I knew from the moment I read the e-mail that I was the one to answer the plea it contained. I'd been looking at my life, and thinking I wanted to do something that would make a difference for someone else. This was my chance. I had to be the one to donate that kidney.

I remember being very calm: in the moment it took me to make my decision, there was no hesitation. It was a surreal feeling. I didn't just want to do it: I had to do it.

I called Steph immediately. I wanted to make sure this decision was okay with her. She told me that when she'd read the e-mail the night before, she'd known I was the one, and that she'd wanted to wake me up and show it to me then. I was so grateful for her support. Steph contacted the family right away, and we started the process.

I spoke with Fran, Mason's mother, and she filled me in on the details of the procedure and talked to me about getting the initial blood work at Jackson Memorial Hospital in Miami. The initial tests proved I was a perfect match for Mason, and over the next ten months I was checked out from top to bottom. I went through psychology and gynecology screenings, CT scans and lung studies. Everything was approved, and the surgery was scheduled for the eve of Rosh Hashanah, in September 2006. I saw this as a good sign: Rosh Hashanah symbolizes the start of a new year, and I wanted to make this a good new year for Mason, a year filled with hope.

Everyone kept asking me if I was nervous, but on the contrary, I couldn't wait for the surgery to happen. The hospital transplant team told me, "If for any reason, you don't want to go through with this, you can back out now." But I only wanted to go forward. I felt that this decision and the surgery itself were something direct from God.

Before surgery, Mason was a non-believer, and very cynical after all the disappointments he'd endured over the course of his struggle to get well. After surgery, when I went in to visit with him in his hospital room, I bent down to kiss him and he said, "There's something to this God thing, you know." That really got me: it was the best feeling. Mason now had hope. He had faith again. And he had a kidney.

During the ten months it took to finish the testing, Mason and I had become good friends. I'd loved him from the moment I first read his mother's e-mail. When I got to really know him, I loved him more. I thought he was a wonderful human being and one of the most brilliant people I'd ever met. He knew just about everything. He was a successful attorney before he became ill, and during the four years of his treatments he'd kept up with work on his computer. He and Stephi have that in common: they're both computer geeks.

More than anything, I loved the closeness of our relationship. I was forty-eight years old and he was the closest thing I had to a child. Of course, he had a mother who had given him life and I couldn't possibly compare myself to her, but I was able to give him a different kind of life. I felt that I had an opportunity to go along with God, and all I had to do was step up to the plate.

People ask me if the surgery was painful, but it ended up being a partial laparoscopic transplant and wasn't that painful at all. Although I remember being in some pain, I don't remember the degree of pain. I would do it again in a heartbeat and wish I had five more kidneys to donate to help others.

It gave me such joy to watch Mason get better. He was transformed. He was laughing again, and he called me with every little medical milestone. "Guess what?" he'd say. "My numbers are up again!" He'd call to tell me about the racquetball game he'd just won, or the softball game he'd just played. And then came the most wonderful call: Mason had fallen in love! He did a lot of living in that first year. He truly got his life back.

Everyone has moments that change his or her life. My moment came when I read that e-mail from Fran. It was so uplifting: I felt like a kid experiencing the joy of Disney World for the first time. I feel so grateful to have met Mason, and I know our meeting was arranged by God.

Moments *do* change lives. If you recognize and are open to your moment, your life will be enriched. It's all about being aware. Today, I'm working as a massage therapist again, using my hands to heal, and I think of Mason every day.

A-A-A: Map the Moment

What was the moment of *Awareness*?

_____

_____

_____

_____

What was the moment of *Acknowledgment*?

_____

_____

_____

_____

What was the *Action* taken?

_____

_____

_____

_____

"Pam is our hero. She's closer than family."

- Fran Steinmark

After our interview was over, Pam Garrett suggested that I speak with Fran Steinmark, Mason's mom. The two women share an incredible bond, appreciation and an enduring love for the man who brought them together.

A Mother's Love and Appreciation

Thoughts from Mason's mother, Fran

We don't know why Mason died. He had been doing so well after his transplant. He'd been active, happy and optimistic about his future, believing in a higher power again, and even falling in love.

The challenges Mason had to endure before his transplant were many. His illness was rare. The outsides of his kidneys had stopped filtering. Though he never overate, he gained over one hundred twenty pounds. It was laborious for him to walk, and his clothes no longer fit. When test after test offered no answers and little hope, Mason began to lose faith in the effectiveness of traditional medicine. Desperate to get well, he tried herbs, teas and oils—but those didn't seem to work either. He was starting to question the power of God.

Finally after one visit to a doctor, it was agreed that he should have his fluids drained with a twenty-four hour lasix drip.

Something happened, we never knew what. Both kidneys failed and Mason was forced to go on dialysis three to four hours a day, three times a week. He didn't do well with this procedure and became very ill, routinely passing out and ending up in the emergency room. He desperately needed a kidney transplant. The most likely candidates, our family, were all considered mismatches by the doctors and ruled out as potential donors. I was told that I had an aneurism, my husband had high blood pressure, and Mason's sister and brother had different blood types.

The long period of time during which one other family member and several friends were tested was an emotional roller coaster. We all knew that Mason was dying, and that he also required a few surgeries while we waited. At that point, he was on a different type of dialysis requiring thirteen and a half hours for the procedure, which meant he had very few hours during the day of "being alive." To me, it seemed like a non-existent life filled with terrible suffering. I was afraid we were going to lose him.

One by one, each potential donor was rejected.

We had one other hope: the National Cadaver List, a transplant waiting list for patients in dire need. Mason was on this list, but each time there was a setback with surgery or emergency hospital visits, his name was dropped further down the list, forcing a delay in receiving a donor kidney.

I'm the chair of a Save Darfur Coalition and work with an interfaith group of wonderful, supportive people. I told them of Mason's situation, and several people came forward to help, but unfortunately they weren't good matches for Mason. Later, we did find a few potential candidates, but despite their good intentions they were not able to complete the process.

Desperate for help, I decided to send out an e-mail to Congregation B'nai Israel, where I had been a member for many years. The cantor, Stephanie, read the e-mail and passed it on to her life partner, Pam. As soon as Pam read the e-mail, she contacted the hospital and scheduled the required testing. She was a perfect match for Mason, both by her blood type and genetically.

Mason was afraid to believe that Pam would actually go through the procedure; after so many false alarms, he simply couldn't handle another rejection. I wanted to ease Mason's fears, so I invited Pam and Stephanie to lunch to meet him. He was terribly afraid, but when the two saw each other for the first time, it was quite emotional. They sobbed in each other's arms. The amount of love in that room was immeasurable; words can't do that meeting justice. Mason was so grateful. He knew he wouldn't make it without Pam's kidney, and he couldn't believe how generous she was in agreeing to go through with the transplant. He felt it was a true miracle.

On the day of surgery, we waited anxiously downstairs. The doctor called us the moment the kidney was transferred from Pam to Mason and again the moment the kidney began to work and filter. It was as if Mason was being born a second time—and this time it was all because of Pam.

Pam's surgery lasted three and a half hours. Mason's surgery lasted seven hours. While Mason was recovering in the emergency ICU, Pam insisted on going to see him, even though she was recovering from surgery herself. She walked with her IV to Mason's room; groggy and on morphine, she leaned over and kissed him.

I said, "Your kidney is keeping him alive."

Pam replied, "No, that's Mason's kidney. I was just holding it for him."

Pam hadn't just given Mason her kidney: she'd given him back his faith. He believed in God again. He was so amazed that a stranger would step forward to save his life out of the goodness of her heart. The love and connection between Mason and Pam was incredible. After the surgeries, they talked every night, sharing things only the two of them could share.

It's hard to describe how we, the family, feel about Pam and Stephanie. Pam is our hero, and she's closer than family. Her gift allowed Mason to lead a real life again. After the surgery, he lost the weight and started playing sports. He started a computer business and fell in love. He was very much alive, so happy and optimistic about the future.

To this day, we don't know why he died. It was devastating to all of us. But I do know that because of Pam's instantaneous decision to give him her kidney, Mason was given a second chance to experience the elation of life.

A-A-A: Map the Moment

What was the moment of *Awareness*?

_____

_____

_____

_____

What was the moment of *Acknowledgment*?

_____

_____

_____

_____

What was the *Action* taken?

_____

_____

_____

_____

4.

Healing Choices

Two Women, Two Diagnoses, Two Choices

"I have come to believe that you should drink your wine, use your fine china, and wear your gold jewelry, because you never know when it can all be taken away."

- Valerie Smaldone

I met popular radio host, writer, and talented performer Valerie Smaldone when she acted as emcee at a Carole Hyatt "Getting To Next" dinner. There, she shared her compelling story of a health scare she had experienced. I was able to interview her a few weeks later.

Her moment is one many women fear and have to face. It came late one night when she arrived home to find a disturbing message on her answering machine. Valerie made a choice in how to deal with her new challenge and was generous enough to share that decision with us.

Drink Your Wine, Use Your Fine China, Wear Your Gold Jewelry

Valerie Smaldone's Story

It took me many months to decide whether to have the minimally invasive surgery known as laparoscopy to remove a cyst from my ovary. I would go back and forth every other month—take out the cyst, don't take it out, take it out, don't take it out. Although I did experience some pain, there didn't seem to be any urgency, and I had a lot going on in my life: in addition to my daily radio show, I was writing a play and working on radio syndication projects. And, even though I wanted to be rid of the pain, I was worried about having the operation.

After six months, near the end of April 2001, I finally decided to have the surgery. During the procedure, the doctor found a growth of abnormal tissue on my uterus, known as endometriosis. He felt this was "a probable cause for my pain," and to be on the safe side he took some additional biopsies. I was back to work a few days after the surgery, feeling relieved, never thinking there would be a further issue.

So that evening, when I heard a message on my answering machine from my doctor saying "Please call me," I was confused. I thought, "Why do I have to call him?" My recovery was going well; I thought everything was fine.

I called the doctor back first thing the next morning, but he wasn't in. When he returned the call, I was on my way to a voice-over audition for *The Today Show*. It was Friday, and the doctor said he wanted to see me first thing on Monday.

"Why can't you tell me what you need to say now?" I asked.

"I have something to discuss with you. I rather not go into detail over the phone," the doctor said.

Not wanting to spend the whole weekend worrying, I insisted, "Please tell me."

At last the doctor said, "The test results show a borderline tumor."

"What does that mean?" I asked.

"That means it could be cancer," he told me.

That moment, those words, changed my life forever.

Somehow, I remained calm. I heard the doctor's words, but nothing he said registered. I remember thinking, "I'm okay! After all, I'm throwing a 50th birthday party for my cousin in just twenty-four hours. I'm working on several syndicated radio shows. I'm busy and active. How could I have cancer?"

I called my sister, who's an oncologist and researcher, and asked her to speak with the doctor. The next time we spoke, I heard her say, "We'll get you through this."

I was officially diagnosed with cancer on April 30, 2001. Three weeks later, I had surgery to remove my right ovary, a procedure called an oopherectomy. I was released from the hospital several days later, on my forty-third birthday. I had held it together all this time, but when I realized I had to have chemotherapy and might lose my hair, I finally broke down in tears. Reality had set in. I had cancer and I had to fight back.

My treatment included a single agent chemotherapy called Carboplatin. Coincidentally, this was a drug my sister had researched and helped develop twenty years before. The treatment took three months. Between June and August, I had four rounds of chemotherapy. With the discomfort came a variety of physical and emotional reactions. Physically, there was nausea, difficulty eating for several days after each treatment, a general overall feeling of weakness and a compromised immune system. I was advised to avoid crowds, to minimize my exposure to germs.

One of the initial routine tests I had to undergo before my surgery was a colonoscopy. The morning of this test, I fainted in the shower, but I had the procedure and then went directly to the emergency room to be treated for a broken ankle. Hobbling around on crutches for many weeks, I felt as if I was being punished for decisions I had made in the past.

Emotionally, I evaluated my life and decisions. I questioned many things. My marriage to a wonderful guy had taken a downward spiral, and there had been a great deal of pain in the breakup of our relationship. Anytime you are the one to initiate the ending of a relationship, or the changing of one, it's hurtful to the one you are leaving as well as to yourself. Now, diagnosed with cancer, I kept thinking, "Am I a terrible person? Do I deserve to be punished?"

The end of August saw my final chemotherapy treatment. Before the diagnosis, I was always so concerned with "should I have said this?" and "should I have done that?" But by the time my chemo was done, I felt foolish about all the time I'd spent being concerned about the minutiae. I cried for that wasted energy and all of my worries about pleasing everyone else... for what?

For the first time, I realized that I couldn't be concerned with what people thought about me, I had to value myself. I had to own who I was. This wasn't about punishment, this was about healing. I began to feel more in control, more focused. If I got angry, fine: for the first time, I vocalized that anger. I also sought alternative methods of healing like acupuncture and yoga, and I concentrated on nutrition. I started to feel better about myself and how I would deal with my future. Death had been a real possibility for me, and now I had to live. I felt as if I was emerging from a cocoon, and I needed to spread my wings differently. I also felt the need to help others empower themselves.

Now, years later, I spend time developing meaningful projects about women in transition. With my writing partner, I continue to work on a play about friendship, and have started a production company to create events and raise awareness for charitable organizations. Throughout the year, I'm invited to speak to oncology and survivors' groups, and I'm honored to do so. My experience has given me a new outlook on living life to the fullest.

Hearing the doctor say the word "cancer" at that moment, and everything that followed as a result, gave me permission to be authentic and express myself as I see fit. Before my diagnosis, you could say I was a hoarder: I was the type of person who held on to my good things, saving them for a special day. But my diagnosis taught me that every day is special. Now, I have come to believe you should drink your wine, use your fine china, and wear your gold jewelry, because you never know when it can all be taken away.

A-A-A: Map the Moment

What was the moment of *Awareness*?

_____

_____

_____

_____

What was the moment of *Acknowledgment*?

_____

_____

_____

_____

What was the *Action* taken?

_____

_____

_____

_____

"I'm living proof that most of the time what you're looking for will not show up as you had expected."

- Lynn Pierce

Professionally, Lynn Pierce describes herself as a "success architect." She helps people discover their passions and create a blueprint for a "life of dreams." Her work as an author and motivational speaker has touched thousands of people.

Lynn's own life has taken many twists and turns, but through it all, the glue which has held her together is the power of spiritual healing.

I met Lynn through a business organization, and soon learned that she—like Valerie Smaldone and so many others—had faced a difficult decision regarding a health crisis. Lynn's moment and subsequent choice in dealing with this dilemma are different than Valerie's, but they share two things in common: courage and encouraging thoughts. Lynn's story is one that gives us a belief in ourselves and in the power each of us holds inside.

Spiritual Healing
Lynn Pierce's Story

As a young girl in Wisconsin, I played office. I was always the office manager. My mother worked in a department store office and I loved going there; I would sit in the big room full of desks and pretend to be the boss.

In high school, I developed an interest in real estate. When I went to the school counselor for advice, I was told, "Look at yourself. You're only eighteen years old, and you don't look a day older than fifteen. No one will ever buy a house from you." Hearing that was a big disappointment, but I listened to the counselor's words. At twenty, I married a struggling young artist. In an effort to support us in our new life together, I went to school for accounting, though I'd never actually considered a career in that field.

The marriage lasted only a few years, the accounting even less. It was then that I went into real estate. It was the 1980s: factories in Wisconsin were closing, and it was hard to sell real estate there. So I started researching where I wanted to work and sell properties. Though I didn't know exactly where I wanted to live, I knew I didn't want cold weather; I wanted to be somewhere warm.

One day, I opened a national real estate magazine and saw an article about Ft. Myers, Florida, which at that time was the number one fastest-growing market in the nation. As soon as I read that article, I decided to move there. I think that was the first time I became aware of designing my own life and recognizing moments that act as catalysts—in this case, opening that magazine at the precise moment I needed that information.

By the age of twenty-four, I had a new life selling real estate in Florida. I traveled, moved a bit around the country, and continued to grow my business, adding clients and professional contacts. A few years later, I remarried, and my husband and I continued to move around the country, including six years in Cabo San Lucas, Mexico, where I worked in sales and management at a popular time share resort.

When I was a child, my family moved about every two years. My father worked for a power company, and we were relocated to a new city with each promotion. I don't think I ever lived in the same place for more than a few years, but now, my husband and I had been in Cabo for almost six years, a record for me. For the first time in my life, I thought we might stay forever.

At that time, I decided to go for my first mammogram. I didn't think anything of it: I was only in my early forties, and life was good. I was healthy, eating a wholesome diet, meditating, enjoying terrific friends and a great lifestyle.

My husband Jeff came with me to my mammogram appointment, since we were going out to dinner with some friends afterward. As soon as they started the test, I knew right away that something was wrong, but since it was my first mammogram I didn't realize how serious the situation was. The technician kept taking more pictures and studying more views. Then, she did an ultrasound scan.

There was a tiny 13" TV screen on the wall where the Spanish-speaking doctor showed me the results. My Spanish is just so-so, but I definitely understood when she said, "This is really bad." It was surreal. There I was in this little room, with only an accordion door separating me from the men waiting for their wives and girlfriends on the other side, looking at that tiny TV and hearing the doctor say, "There's something there." It was hard to process.

I went out, told Jeff, and brought him in to see the test results. When we left the office it was about five o'clock; as we walked out into the light of day, I remember thinking, "This is the same door I walked in a short time ago, but now everything is different." I can still see that scene in my mind; see everything that was around me, all 360 degrees, like I was in the middle of a circle. It was this exact moment that I believe changed my life—not the moment I was told I had cancer, but the moment I walked out into the light and knew that somehow I would make it through.

As we approached our car, I remember telling Jeff, "I don't think this is the end. But if for any reason it is, I'm ready to move away now. It's time for us to go." It was an unusual time for me to move away from a successful career and a place I'd finally planted roots. We'd been fortunate enough to be able to buy a lot of property in Cabo San Lucas, and I also had blueprints for houses I had designed. We had been planning to live in that beautiful spot permanently. But in the moment I walked out of the clinic and into the sunlight, I knew I was done there.

I said to Jeff: "There is a huge lesson for me in this diagnosis. I haven't just been hit with a pebble, there's a big boulder knocking me over. I have to figure out how to get back up, and figure out what I can learn from this experience so I can get through it as quickly as possible." I didn't cry. I didn't panic. I just started to process how to handle this, so I could learn the lesson and find the quickest path to the other side.

We didn't belong to a church in Cabo, but I did attend a weekly spiritual discussion group. I felt that if I really believed in the spiritual healing we talked about each week, this was the time to put into practice. I went to my bookcase to see if any of the mind/body healing books I had been studying for almost twenty years contained information on how to get through this challenge.

I wasn't big on Western medicine, but did believe in alternative Eastern practices. I called an iridologist, someone who could look into my eyes and see if there was any indication that my organs were unhealthy. I told her I had been diagnosed with breast cancer and needed a second opinion, and asked her to help prepare me if the second opinion came back with the same diagnosis. I asked her for supplements, advice on diet, and suggestions about changes I needed to make to rid myself of toxins. In anticipation of any possible surgery, I wanted my body in the best place possible.

I had worked with several charities during my time in Cabo. One in particular flew in volunteer doctors to help poor families get medical treatment. A friend of mine was a nurse, and she suggested I speak with a certain specialist who was flying in that week. I took my mammogram films to him, and he suggested that I see a leading cutting-edge surgeon in Salt Lake City.

When I called to make an appointment with the surgeon, I was given a date four weeks later. Jeff and I usually vacationed in Colorado, but that year, coincidentally, I had booked a hotel for us in Utah during the exact week my new medical appointment was scheduled.

I had a month before I had to see the specialist, so I went to see another doctor for a second opinion, as I'd planned. I was told that a lumpectomy, chemotherapy, radiation and drains in my breast would be necessary. This doctor wanted to schedule this surgery immediately.

I had friends who'd chosen to go the surgical route, and thankfully they are healthy now, but I had a feeling that this path was not for me. Instead, I decided to quit my job and make my body my full-time job. I wanted to get as healthy as possible. That decision marked a big turning point in my life. I was a very successful real estate agent in a profession that was male-dominated at that time. I was making a great deal of money and doing very well. But my health was more important to me.

My regimen consisted of meditation, yoga, affirmation tapes, acupuncture, hypnosis, and herbs. A friend of mine even brought me to see a healer who lived on an Indian reservation and used eagle feathers, sage, and smoke to help heal me. I tried every alternative therapy I could find.

After two weeks, I thought I was doing a very good job and went back to the doctor for another ultrasound. I really thought the lump would be smaller—but no, it was exactly the same. It was then that I started to panic. My alternative plan was not working. I'd thought I could make it all go away. I called the iridologist again and said, "Let's get me ready for surgery in two weeks." I kept doing what I had been doing and restricted my diet even more, eliminating wine, cheese, meat, and mushrooms, and eating mostly fresh food.

Two weeks later, Jeff and I left for our vacation and for my appointment with the highly-regarded surgeon in Salt Lake City. When I walked into his office, the first thing he said to me was, "You don't have cancer. The people in my office waiting room, they're dying. But I would be shocked if you have cancer."

I had brought a list of the vitamins and herbs I was taking. I thought, "He's going to think I'm some whacko!" But he was fine with alternative therapy. He said, "Let's do another mammogram now and compare the films." This was my third time now looking at the images on the screen, and I couldn't believe what was on the monitor. He showed me the lump. This time it was not solid. There was just a shell, with no tumor inside! He looked at the other mammograms and read the reports from the first two doctors. I couldn't believe what I was hearing as he confirmed that the lump was almost totally gone.

Leaving that office with Jeff and once again stepping out into the light was a totally different experience. It was amazing. I was so relieved. There would be no surgery. It was an affirmation of everything I believed. My spiritual beliefs had never really been tested before, but now they most certainly had, and they were stronger for it.

When I heard the first breast cancer diagnosis, I stayed true to my spiritual leanings and didn't run scared. I followed a path that I felt was right for me. Fortunately, I had people in my life with similar beliefs who were able to support me. Even my decision to get that first mammogram was due to a friend's comment at dinner. At that time, a mammogram hadn't been in my thoughts, but then a business associate also suggested that I get one. I remember thinking that when a third person, someone you don't know well, tells you something so personal, it's a spiritual message that should be followed.

The day I received that first diagnosis, I had a sense that it was time to leave Mexico, that there was something bigger I was supposed to do with my life. I didn't know then what it was, but I knew it was time to move on, and we did.

From Mexico we moved to Arizona. I don't know why I chose the desert after living in a beach community, but I had a feeling that area of the country would be good for Jeff and me. One day, I felt a pull to attend a particular discussion. The speaker talked about a program he was creating which would help thousands of people become millionaires. Though there were five hundred people in that room that day, I was the only person who signed up. Not only did I sign up, I came back home and announced that I was going to write a book. I had been waiting for a sign, week after week, for eleven months, a signal to show me what to do next in my life. And now it had come.

The action I took to attend a talk that day ended up giving my life a purpose. The speaker was Mark Victor Hansen, co-author of *Chicken Soup for the Soul*, and he has been an angel in my life. When he spoke about the program he was initiating to help create millionaires, I felt as if I was in suspended animation and he was talking only to me. Before that day, I had always been in sales, but after that talk, I knew what I was going to do: I was going to write a book for women. I came home elated. I started getting up very early in the morning to write. I couldn't stop writing! Not only did I write that book, I have written several more.

When I speak, I tell people my story, and talk about how sometimes it's necessary to step out of your comfort area. You may not have an idea of what you want to do with your life, you may not have a vision of how to make it happen, your eyes may not be open to possibilities, you may have a preconceived notion of how things should be or how things are going to work out... but then something happens unexpectedly, and your life changes.

Walking out into the light of Cabo San Lucas on the day of my diagnosis, I knew I was starting on a different journey, one that had taken me totally by surprise. That moment changed the direction of my life. Today I'm a writer, a speaker and a success architect. I help others discover their passions and live their dreams. This is a totally unexpected career path for me, but I love what I do. I'm aware of the defining moments that have helped shape my future and define my life, and I try to stay open to things from unanticipated sources. I'm living proof that most of the time what you're looking for will not show up as you expected.

A-A-A: Map the Moment

What was the moment of *Awareness*?

_____

_____

_____

What was the moment of *Acknowledgment*?

_____

_____

_____

What was the *Action* taken?

_____

_____

_____

_____

5.

Prayerful

Two Neighbors, Two Prayerful Moments

"I had doubt for quite a while. Now, my doubt has turned to belief."

- Lisa Hauptman

Arleen and Larry Blocksberg were neighbors of mine in South Florida. Coincidentally, we all moved to New York City and now live a few blocks from each other. At dinner one night with their family, I mentioned my book project, and their daughter, Lisa, told me about a moment in a taxi cab which helped restore her hope of becoming a mother and renewed her diminishing faith.

Finding a Wallet, Finding Faith
Lisa Hauptman's Story

For the most part, my life was comfortable and happy. I managed a law firm specializing in the music industry. My husband Robby and I led active, social lives. But our good fortune didn't seem to extend to what we wanted most: a family.

We tried for months, but I couldn't get pregnant. Robby and I decided to try in-vitro fertilization, but a year and a half later, we still weren't seeing results. I was very unhappy, partly due to all the hormones I was taking, partly due to a feeling of not being in control. Even though this was my body, I couldn't make the pregnancy stick. The desire to get pregnant, and my sense of despair when it didn't happen, had taken over my life. When I wasn't thinking about getting pregnant, I was dealing with not being pregnant.

Out with friends one day, I listened as one friend talked about the problems her boyfriend was having at work. He owned a bar, and had discovered that one of his employees was stealing from him, so he had set up cameras around the bar to catch the thief in the act. Hearing this, my first reaction was to say, "I don't understand people like that. How could anyone steal? I mean, if I found a wallet with $4,000 inside, I'd do everything I could to find the owner and give the money back."

The very next day, I left work to go to the hospital for one of the routine blood tests that were part of my fertility program. I hailed a cab to take me uptown, and after a few minutes of driving through traffic, my elbow poked something in the backseat. There was a very expensive Louis Vuitton backpack lying on the seat next to me. Curious, I opened the bag; there was a matching wallet inside. I knew how much the wallet was worth even without its contents, because I'd recently looked at one in the store, only to find it was well out of my price range; all of our money was going to my fertility treatments now.

Inside the wallet was a stack of hundred-dollar bills. I counted them: there were forty, $4,000 in all. A little shocked, I looked out the window and up to the sky and said, "Are you kidding? You didn't believe me."

I was certain this was a test, a chance for me to prove what I'd said the day before. And just to sweeten the pot, a higher being decided to throw in the pricey wallet I'd wanted, too—like He was saying, "That's right, let's see what you do now!"

In the hospital waiting room, I went through the bag to see if it contained an ID, or something else that could help me find the person who owned it. I also called my friend, the one whose boyfriend owned the bar.

"You're never going to believe what just happened," I told her. "I just found a wallet on the seat of a taxi cab, and it had $4,000 in it!"

"No way!" my friend said. "I can't believe it!"

When I got off the phone, I continued searching through the bag. While I did find a student ID from NYU, there was no address, no phone number, and no cell phone. The card showed a photo of a young Asian girl, eighteen years old, with an identification number on the back. I decided to call the University to see if they could track her down. I told the receptionist at the school what had happened, and left them my phone number in case anyone reported the bag missing. Then, I returned to my office, bag in hand.

As soon as I sat down, the phone rang. It was the police department. The young woman had gone there to make a claim, and while she'd been filling out the report, her cell phone rang—the University, calling to say her bag had been found. The officer I was speaking to told me that the girl was right in front of him, and I asked him to have her identify something in the bag, just to be sure. And yes, the bag was hers.

The student and her sister came right over to my office. Since the girl was just learning English, her sister did most of the talking. When I handed over the bag and the girl saw that all of her money was still there, she started to cry. The older sister started to hand me a stack of hundred-dollar bills as a reward, but I declined. After all, this was my test.

"It will come back to me," I told her.

In that conversation with my friend, I'd arbitrarily chosen the figure of $4,000. I'd just picked a random number, a huge number to me, a sum that was big enough to make a difference in someone's life. A sum that, if lost and then returned, would mean something.

It's not every day you get to make a difference in a stranger's life. I felt that I had given that young student faith in humanity. I had also passed my test: I'd found a wallet full of cash, and done what I had to do to return it, just like I'd said I would. I felt great, as if I had won the lottery.

I feel now that that moment in my life, that test, has restored my faith as well. That amazing incident had to be more than just coincidence.

It had to be the result of a higher power watching over me. There's no explaining it otherwise.

Life went on from there. Still in the midst of the fertility program, Robby and I tried again to conceive. I kept thinking that, if I were to have a baby, it would be best reward of all for returning that wallet. But it didn't happen. So I decided to lay off the treatments for a while and focus on restoring my body. I also thought that maybe I should begin helping other women with their fertility issues. After all, I knew a lot about fertility at this point.

Several months went by, and Robby and I decided to try again. And again, nothing happened. This meant more cancelled IVF attempts and another emotional roller coaster ride for me. I was very sad, so I decided to go for a massage to help myself unwind a little. Speaking with the masseur, I discovered that he and his wife had experienced problems in conceiving as well. He said they'd tried for years, until a friend came to town and told them that they had to visit the Shrine of Saint Jude in Baltimore, and pray there. "St. Jude is invoked in prayer when all else seems hopeless," their friend told them.

The masseur and his wife followed their friend's advice. They were pregnant soon after.

Robby and I decided to try it as well. After all, what did we have to lose? That summer, we went to Baltimore with friends for a fun weekend and while we were there visited the shrine. Despite all our recent disappointments, my faith was stronger after finding that wallet, and I prayed with my whole heart.

In March, we finally heard the news we'd been waiting for. My pregnancy test came back positive. I finally heard the doctor say, "You are pregnant!" We were having a baby! All the waiting, all the disappointments, suddenly didn't matter anymore. They had been worth it.

Finding that wallet triggered a domino effect in my life. Since then, it seems like everything I've been given has been exactly what I wanted. Although I doubted it for a long time, a higher power was taking care of me, watching over me. Now, I have a renewed faith, and a beautiful baby girl named Lindsay whom I love more than I ever thought possible.

A-A-A: Map the Moment

What was the moment of *Awareness*?

_____

_____

_____

_____

What was the moment of *Acknowledgment*?

_____

_____

_____

_____

What was the *Action* taken?

_____

_____

_____

_____

"I got down on my knees and prayed. I said, 'I have a problem and can't come out of this by myself.'"

- Lamberto Dominici

Lamberto Dominici is a neighbor of mine. We live in the same apartment building. One morning as we rode down in the elevator, he told me that he had a moment to share with me.

Lamberto's moment came in the middle of summer. Business was extremely slow for his designer import showroom in midtown Manhattan. Steady customers were away on vacation, and each day less than a handful of shoppers stopped in to browse, or buy one of the colorful Italian leather handbags, accessories or designer dresses. In his six years as owner/manager, Lamberto had never seen business this bad.

Sales were barely totaling $500 a day when three men in trench coats walked in to his showroom flashing their IRS badges. What followed was the moment that brought Lamberto to his knees in prayer.

Power of Prayer
Lamberto Dominici's Story

"Lamberto, you owe the IRS $12,400," the men with badges said. "Either give us a check or in one hour our locksmith will close this place down."

I knew I owed the government money, but each day I hoped business would turn around for the better. As I stood there frozen in the middle of my showroom, unable to move, I was petrified. I could lose the company I had worked so hard to build.

The IRS officers proceeded to walk over and tell my customers and salespeople to leave because they were seizing the property. I just stood there thinking, "What am I going to do?"

Embarrassed that my staff and my customers had to see this happening, I finally asked the men to step into my office, where they presented me with the IRS bill totaling exactly $12,400. I knew that I had little money in the bank—maybe under $1000, certainly not enough to pay the bill—but in an effort to stall for time, I told the officers I needed to call my bank to get the exact balance in my account.

To my utter amazement, the bank official on the line told me that my balance was $13,000! While the IRS men waited in my office, I ran to the bank to get a certified check.

As I handed the men that check for $12,400, I thought, "How is this possible? Where did this money come from?" A depressing $500 per day from sales was all I had to cover payroll. How could I have $13,000 in my bank account?

An hour later, the answer to this mystery was revealed. I received a phone call from my cousin and business partner in Italy.

"Ciao, Lamberto," my cousin said. "Yesterday I wired $12,000 to your bank. I purchased a painting at Sotheby's, and now I need you to make a check out for that amount and pick up the painting for me."

"Oh no," I thought, "That's where the money came from." I was so ashamed of my IRS problem, and of what I'd done with my cousin's money, that I thought I would die.

I needed time to calm down and gather the courage to tell my cousin the truth, and said I would call him tomorrow. I was desperate. It was the lowest point of my life, and to top it off, by stalling, I felt like such a baby. Here I was, a grown man, not facing my problem. Over and over again, I asked myself, "What am I going to do? What am I going to do?"

Before going to sleep that night, I got down on my knees and prayed.

"I have a problem I cannot solve," I told God. "I can't come out of this by myself."

The next morning, I got to my store earlier than usual. In six years of operation, I had never opened up before 10:00 a.m., but I began that day at 9:00 a.m. No sooner had I opened the door when the first customer came in. I hadn't even taken off my coat!

Business continued like that all morning and afternoon. Customers streamed in all day. We were so busy that I had no time during the day to appreciate or realize fully what was happening.

That whole summer I hadn't sold more than $500 a day, but on that day we made $12,400—yes, $12,400! Almost to the penny, I made the exact amount I needed. I had prayed for help and that's exactly what I received.

The following day, I went to the bank and deposited the thousands of dollars. Then, I walked over to Sotheby's, wrote a check for the amount of purchase, and arranged for the shipping of my cousin's painting.

To me, what happened couldn't be anything but a miracle. It seemed incredible that when I called the bank, I was told I had enough money in my account to pay the IRS bill, but I believe the truly miraculous moment was the one of prayer, when I got on my knees and asked for help. That moment not only produced a solution to my desperate money problem, it brought forth my faith. It was prayer that helped me make over $12,000 that day. For the remainder of the summer, I never once made more than $500 a day in sales, but my business was safe, and I had a renewed belief in the power of prayer.

A-A-A: Map the Moment

What was the moment of *Awareness*?

_____

_____

_____

_____

What was the moment of *Acknowledgment*?

_____

_____

_____

_____

What was the *Action* taken?

_____

_____

_____

_____

6.

Loss and Inspiration

"In the midst of difficulty lies opportunity."
- Attributed to Albert Einstein [4]

Three Women, Three Mothers, Three Losses: Three lessons in how tragedy can lead a special person to inspire others.

"I see it as two sides to a coin. On one side, there's that moment of unspeakable and horrifying loss, one that no one should have to go through. And on the other side, there's a moment that enables you to somehow find what is needed to go on."

- Liz Neumark

My friend Gina Rogak invited me to a rather lavish catering event: several hundred guests all there for a delicious food tasting, hosted by one catering company, Great Performances. When we left the event, we were given a "goody bag." Included inside were some brochures from the caterer about an organization called The Sylvia Center. Having written and produced hundreds of human interest stories for television, I had a sense that there might be a special moment here for my book, so I called the caterer.

As it turns out, Liz Neumark is a very busy woman. Besides operating Great Performances, which has a twenty-five year contract at the prestigious Plaza Hotel, she runs the Mae Mae Café, a charming space in Soho, and founded Katchkie Farm in upstate New York. This farm is home to an educational organization, The Sylvia Center, and it's here on this sixty-acre organic farm that her heart soars.

Liz's passion for this project and for farming is the result of one unthinkable loss. Named for Liz's daughter, The Sylvia Center has come to represent joy and compassion, and captures the essence of a special child: Sylvia, "a helpful human."

Sylvia, A Helpful Human
Liz Neumark's Story

Almost thirty years ago, a friend and I started a business which we called Great Performances. My partner had been a dancer, and I had visions of becoming a photographer. Our company hired struggling young performers who needed the wages as they pursued their careers. Our goal was to work with catering companies and offer a "waitress staffing service" for women in the arts.

Though I hadn't been trained in catering, service was big in my home. My mom taught us to serve properly, even at our own dinner table. I remember her advice: "Serve from the left and clear from the right." Eventually, as the staffing business grew and we covered more events, we added men to our employee list and expanded our services to include catering. Working with caterers was on-the-job training for us; watching them, we learned a great deal about what was involved in planning and executing events. We were fortunate to take on more and more clients, and soon we officially became a catering company.

After years of catering, you can become very conscious of the urgency of each event and get caught up in the details. You begin to ask yourself, "Is the green salad just the right color? Are the flower arrangements perfectly placed?" Each element takes on paramount proportions, and it's easy to lose sight of fundamentals.

I'm a city kid: I grew up in New York City with cement under my feet. I graduated from college with a degree in Urban Affairs. But I had begun to dream about having my own farm, which to me represented the true building blocks of life: the earth, a seed, and the growth that follows. Whether it's a business, financial or family situation, if the root is strong everything is strong. As our company grew, I knew that it was important to focus on the things which were at the root of our business: fresh, high-quality food, unique flavors, and great customer service.

In short, life seemed to be going very well—until one horrifying moment changed everything.

One Saturday night, my husband, my four children and I went to a neighborhood community party. Everyone was having fun, when the youngest of our children, six year old Sylvia, began complaining of a headache. Her pain escalated very quickly, and she lost consciousness. When we got to the hospital, the doctors told us that Sylvia had suffered a sudden aneurism. She died two days later.

As I mentioned, I'd been living in a world of catering detail, where close attention is paid to every minor placement of a knife and fork, and agitation can erupt over something as small as the wrong greens placed in a salad. Losing Sylvia totally changed my perspective. At the end of the day, I began to wonder, what did it matter?

I experienced such grief that I didn't think I could ever come back. But I held on to an idea. The thought of farming somehow brought me peace of mind. I began to participate in CSA membership gardening, which is Community-Supported Agriculture. When an individual buys a farm share, the money enables the farmer to operate his or her farm, and the shareholders get a percentage of the farm's yields each week. It's a win-win situation. I became a "CSA junkie," and soon I had several memberships.

My healing began on these farms. I was suffering such unbelievable grief, but on the farms, I found a place to console myself. It was as if something clicked inside me. I can't explain it, but the farm represented life, because here, the earth provided living things. Despite what I had suffered, as I sat and watched vegetables grow, I witnessed life going on and knew I could still be a part of it and contribute to the process. The farms became safe places for me, and I did a great deal of thinking there.

When older people die, as devastating as that death can be to their family, they leave behind a legacy, a whole life to be remembered. People talk about them, relive their experiences with them. But when children die, people are afraid to talk about them, or about their deaths. They're so afraid to add to your family's grief, to make you feel even sadder. But even though hearing Sylvia's name made me cry, I wanted people to say it. I wanted to hear my daughter's name.

Sylvia brought more joy and intensity into her short life than some people experience in a lifetime. She loved to help others and was always thinking of ways to give. She loved bringing gifts to her friends. Animals gave her particular joy, and she enjoyed taking care of them. Remembering all the wonderful things about Sylvia's life, I knew I had to do two things: I had to give my daughter a legacy, and I had to say her name.

As time went on, I began to realize that I had to buy a farm. It would be a place of comfort, a place where my family and I could begin again. We could plant seeds and watch things grow. I knew that once we had this farm, we could give Sylvia a legacy. We would be able to say her name again.

It took us a few years to find the right property, but in 2006 we finally did. Katchkie Farm in upstate New York has several acres of woods; a two-acre pond teeming with fish, frogs and turtles; and sprawling fields where we grow a variety of products. Pumpkins, flowers and beets are plentiful. Seasonally, we grow what we call our "garden lasagna"—tomatoes, peppers, eggplant, onions, garlic, zucchini and cucumbers. We also have three large greenhouses where we grow salad greens all winter. People often ask me how we named the farm. "Katchkie" is a term of endearment I gave my son when he was born.

Our farm became the home of The Sylvia Center, a place where kids can come together to have fun, learn about farming, help with the harvest, and cook healthy and nutritious food for their families. It's a place to connect children with joyful food experiences, and where I can feel connected to Sylvia. I know Sylvia would have been first in line at all the activities.

We have a counterpart in the city, too, with our Kids' Kitchen, where city children come for cooking lessons. We have an education division that coordinates with the school classrooms and green markets, and to spread the word, we've partnered with several organizations including Big Brother and Big Sisters, New York Cares, The Mayor's Office of Volunteers, city schools and others. Children have fun in the Kids' Kitchen doing things that Sylvia would have loved.

It's important for my family to know we began a program that connects us to Sylvia's spirit. Life changed in one devastating moment. Knowing that our farm has come from her makes my moment in time a paradox. It has been four years now, and the pain and loss hasn't left me, yet I feel that the human spirit is very powerful. I'm lucky that Sylvia has given me the power to pay tribute to her, and I know that she knows I'm grateful for that. I see it as two sides to a coin. On one side, there's that moment of unspeakable and horrifying loss, one that no one should have to go through. And on the other side, there's a moment that enables you to somehow find what is needed to go on.

Now we talk about Sylvia often, and about her bright life and loving nature. She's with us, and we have captured her essence through the Center. Now, we can say her name. We have given her a legacy. That's Sylvia being a helpful human.

A-A-A: Map the Moment

What was the moment of *Awareness*?

_____

_____

_____

_____

What was the moment of *Acknowledgment*?

_____

_____

_____

_____

What was the *Action* taken?

_____

_____

_____

_____

"I came to understand that many of us live with broken hearts. But when you touch broken hearts together, a new heart emerges, one that is more open and compassionate, one able to touch others: a heart that seeks God."

- Sherri Mandell

In November of 2001, I travelled to the Middle East as a producer with a crew from WCBS-TV. Our assignment was to get a sense of what people there were thinking about America and Americans. We travelled to Egypt, Jordan, Kuwait, Dubai and Israel. The reporter, Lou Young, interviewed a mother in Israel who had recently lost a child. The woman's name was Sherri Mandell.

After returning to the United States, I continually thought about her story and her agonizing moment. A few weeks before submitting my manuscript to the publisher, I was able to interview her.

Nothing in Sherri's past could have prepared her for the loss of her son. It's a moment no parent should have to endure—but it was a moment that started her on her personal spiritual journey, and enabled her to honor a beloved one and help many others in the process. Her story—which is fully and beautifully told in her book, *The Blessing of a Broken Heart*—will stay with you, and make you think about ways in which you can make a difference in the lives of others. In this story, I have included both Sherri's thoughts from our interview and passages from her touching book.[5]

A Spiritual Journey
Sherri Mandell's Story

Growing up on Long Island, my initial career plan was to be a flight attendant, known as a stewardess back then. I'm not sure why I chose that profession, since I hated flying, but it seemed glamorous. Like many other young women in my generation, another goal was to marry one of the Beatles. Neither one happened.

After graduating college and getting my Masters degree in writing, I taught at several colleges. One year, I took a trip to visit a friend in Israel, where I met Seth, a fellow American and my future husband. I stayed in Israel, resuming my studies there, and we married in Jerusalem in 1985. Our first two children were born in Israel, but after several years we moved back to the United States. Seth had always been more observant than I: at that time, I didn't think I was ready to be an Israeli, and I wanted to be closer to my family.

We had two more children in the seven years we stayed in the United States. I was very busy being a mom and spending time with friends and family. Seth, who is a rabbi, became executive director of Hillel in College Park, Maryland and a director at Penn State University Hillel.

Eventually, though, we decided to move back to Israel and raise our children as Israelis. We planted ourselves in a loving, strong community where families were both religious and secular. The school, too, had a diversity that we liked. The people we met were beautiful souls, and the landscape was stunning. The friendships we made here helped me decide that this was where I wanted to live and raise my family.

Though we were far from our families in the United States, we had good friends and a sense that our children were happy and healthy. It seemed to be a throwback to a 1950s environment: here, kids played outside with friends from morning till evening, no play dates were necessary, and we kept our doors open at all times.

But all that changed on May 8, 2001.

Our oldest son, Koby, was thirteen years old, a few weeks shy of his fourteenth birthday. Koby and a neighborhood boy named Yosef Ish-Ran had become good friends. Koby had moved back to Israel in fourth grade and still retained American interests. He kept up with American sports, collected baseball cards, and loved Cal Ripken. He was brilliant in school, and had a photographic memory which helped him with some difficulties he had in learning Hebrew.

Yosef was his first Israeli friend with whom he could speak Hebrew. Koby was a little shy; Yosef was very social, more gregarious than Koby, but they were always laughing when they were together. One of the things that must have drawn Koby and Yosef together was their sense of humor and love of jokes.

On that day in May, Koby and Yosef decided to play hooky from school. They stopped at our local grocery, picked up some supplies, and headed out on an excursion. They must have been looking for adventure when they chose to explore a canyon close to home, just a five minute walk from our house. Their destination—the *wadi*, as it is called—is amazingly beautiful. It's a dry river bed with hiking trails that lead to the Dead Sea, exotic caves housing ruins which date back to the fifth century, and breathtaking views of rugged mountains and olive groves.

The day started out as normal. Yosef came by to pick Koby up at 7:20 a.m. I had made Koby two salami sandwiches for his lunch. After they left for school, I left to go swimming, had a few meetings in town and then worked on editing a manuscript for a friend. Seth had an assignment as a freelance business writer and was working from home, so there was no need for me to worry about the children coming home to an empty house. I called the house a few times and Seth told me that all the children were out. Each day, they'd come home from school, drop off their bags, and go right back out to play basketball, be with friends or attend an afternoon youth group activity.

When I returned home around 6:00 p.m., I asked Seth, "Where's Koby?" My middle son, Daniel, was on an overnight school trip so he was not home and wouldn't know. My daughter, Eliana, came home from youth group around 8:30 p.m.; she said she hadn't seen Koby all day. I put Gavi and Eliana to sleep and there was still no sign of Koby.

It was then that the worry started. I called different friends. One of them said that perhaps the boys had gone to Jerusalem for a demonstration. Another mother told me that one of the roads had been closed. I convinced myself that it was just taking them longer than usual to get home, and that Koby would walk in soon. Also, it was Tuesday, so he could have gone to a weekly youth group meeting. Yosef's mom was convinced that they were at the demonstration. There were several reasonable explanations for their being late. But by 10:00 p.m., I was frantic.

At 11:00 p.m., I called the police. Another neighbor called Koby's teacher, and we found out that Koby and Yosef hadn't been in school that day. I tried to remain calm. I knew Koby was with Yosef and they would be home soon. When a friend of Koby's came over and told us that the two boys had planned to go to the wadi, I remember still thinking they would be home soon.

All night, our neighbors stayed with us to offer moral support. They told us, "Welcome to the teen years. We've all been through this." I wanted to believe them: I couldn't accept that Koby wasn't safe, but he had never done anything like this before and would usually come home by 6:00 p.m. I knew he wouldn't worry us like this. I just wanted him to walk in the door so that I could yell at him for being naughty. Some of our neighbors shared stories of their children who had gotten lost in surrounding caves and had subsequently been found safe. I took some comfort in knowing the caves are very big and it would have certainly been easy to get lost in them.

By 4:00 a.m., Seth and I went looking for the boys. We couldn't find them. I felt my legs begin to buckle, but I still felt he would come home. I am now pleading with God and Koby. The boys need to come home now. Come back now. Come back now! I paced in front of the house and Seth went to the synagogue, hoping his prayers would bring the boys home.

My friends were all around me when another friend, Shira, walked into my house. She looked at me, took my hand in hers and said: "They found them. They're dead." Friends tell me that I fainted. I just remember crying and holding Seth.

Koby and Yosef had gone exploring that day. They were murdered, stoned to death. They were just thirteen and fourteen years old, and their lives were taken from us forever. Though their murderers were never found, the act was attributed to Palestinian terrorists. Two wonderful boys killed, their deaths demonstrating the hatred between different people.

I just held on to Seth and cried. I couldn't stop the tears. I didn't know how I could survive this loss. Seth was a rabbi and I looked to him for help. Immediately Seth said that we had three other children, and somehow we would not let this horrific tragedy ruin their lives.

I could have stayed in bed the rest of my life mourning Koby. My friends tried to relieve my pain. They stayed with us day and night, offering love and whatever help they could give. But I couldn't stop crying.

Since I'm a professional writer, one of my friends suggested that I write about Koby using a free-form style called "automatic writing," which had been shown to be successful in dealing with emotional pain. My friend suggested that I use my writing to have a conversation with Koby. Since I was left-handed, she explained that I should write with my right hand; somehow this reversal technique allows feelings and non-expressed thoughts to surface and begin to flow.

I tried it. With my tears streaming, I would write and cry, write and cry. It was painful, but I kept doing it, and amazingly, this style of writing helped. I'm not sure I understand exactly what happened, but in writing with my right hand, I was able to express what I was feeling and speak directly to Koby.

And remarkably, Koby spoke to me. In one conversation, I heard him say, "Do something to make children feel good about themselves." Our family had been thinking about how to honor Koby: now we had an answer and a direction.

The summer after Koby was killed, we thought it would be good for our children to have a change of environment, so we sent them to sleep-away camp in America. It was hard for them. Daniel called home crying, saying he couldn't stop thinking how much Koby would have liked camp.

It was difficult to hear Daniel so upset, but now we knew what we had to do. We needed to heal our family and honor Koby, and a camp seemed to be the perfect way to do that. We wanted to do something he would have liked, something which had his spirit. We also knew that there was no camp for kids like ours, children who had suffered and survived a personal loss due to a terrorist killing. These children need to talk, but often they don't do so, because they feel guilty and don't want to add to the grief of their parents or surviving parent.

We started Camp Koby to provide direct and indirect therapy. We offer art, drama, yoga, and plain old American-style fun. Our first year, we thought maybe thirty kids would show up: we had one hundred and fifty. By the next summer, four hundred campers, aged eight to eighteen, participated in our program, and the following summer our numbers rose to six hundred. The programs at Camp Koby are all free, and some continue throughout the school year.

The Koby Mandell Foundation was founded in 2002 to honor Koby and Yosef. Along with the camp, it has now grown to include a Big Brother/Big Sister follow-up program, and healing retreats for families and women. Those affected by terrorist activities can get away for a three-day holiday. Healing groups for children, teens, mothers and fathers are offered, along with hiking, kayaking, and other fun activities.

As a rabbi and Hillel director, Seth has a great deal of experience initiating student programs, and now he supervises the activities of the Foundation. For me, my spirituality has grown, as have my positive feelings about raising my family in Israel.

Since that terrifying day when Koby disappeared, amazing spiritual things have occurred in my life. When you go through such a tragedy, it takes you out of time, and that time becomes eternity. The person who is gone loses a sense of time. Koby would be twenty-one now, but is he still thirteen? It becomes more than a moment, it becomes an eternal moment. And with that, momentum: in our case, momentum to start a program to give Koby a voice and capture his spirit. It's paradoxical how the profound loss of Koby has made life more meaningful.

I knew I would have to write about Koby and this awakening. During our shiva and extended mourning for our son, friends and family sat around telling stories about Koby. He was so bright, thoughtful, loving and funny. I will always long for Koby and feel the pain of his absence, but I have come to realize that it is possible to rebuild a new heart, which at first I thought would be impossible to replace. One summer after camp, my daughter told me that she had liked camp so much because "It's like we touched each others' hearts. We put our hearts together, and we made a new heart." Touched by her words, I called my book *The Blessing of a Broken Heart*.

My journey from enormous grief to reaching out to help others started with one agonizing moment: the moment I heard that my firstborn and his best friend had been stoned to death. In chronicling this journey, I have come to understand that many of us live with broken hearts. But when you touch broken hearts together, a new heart emerges, one that is more open and compassionate, one able to touch others: a heart that seeks God. That is the blessing of a broken heart.

A-A-A: Map the Moment

What was the moment of *Awareness*?

_____

_____

_____

_____

What was the moment of *Acknowledgment*?

_____

_____

_____

_____

What was the *Action* taken?

_____

_____

_____

_____

"I believe people can go through pain, heal, and then try to discover what they were supposed to learn from that experience."

- Dottie Herman

For over a decade, I had taken steps to write and complete this book. Because producing for television is so time-consuming, I had to put the project aside for long periods of time. But when my mother, who was my major supporter, died, I became determined to see it through. I knew I couldn't take on a seven–day-a-week producing job and still continue to research, interview, write and edit. At that time, a cousin of mine suggested I help her with her real estate customers, since this would afford me the time I needed to write as well.

Oops! Turns out, real estate also is a six- to seven-day-a-week job. I also found out that the people who work in this field are dedicated professionals. Leading that list of individuals is Dottie Herman, CEO and President of one of the nations' leading real estate companies, Prudential Douglas Elliman. She was named one of the "100 Most Influential Women in New York" by Crain's *New York Business,* and chosen as one of *Fortune Magazine's* "Most Powerful Women."

I was immediately impressed with Dottie and attended several of her educational seminars; each time, I came away with a feeling that this was a woman who cared deeply about her company and the people in it. I felt there had to be a moment that helped shaped her managerial skills, and there was: a devastating childhood loss that helped shape who she has become today and enabled her to overcome adversity with a positive outlook and nurturing spirit.

A Childhood Loss

Dottie Herman's Story

When I was ten years old, my mother was killed on the way home from a family ski vacation.

I'm the eldest of three children. At that time, my younger brother was eight and my sister was four. We had just left my mother's friend's house in Vermont, and were headed home to Long Island when we hit a terrible ice storm. My mother was suffering from a migraine headache, and needed to get off the road to rest, so my dad veered off the parkway. As he was pulling over, our car skidded on the ice, flipped and then exploded.

This was the 1960s, before we all wore seat belts. I was sitting directly behind my mother and the two of us were thrown from the car. I was knocked out and do not remember what happened. My mom was also thrown, but she hit her head on a rock, and died instantly. When our car flipped over, the gasoline tank burst and my brother and sister were burned all over their bodies. Miraculously, though, today they have no physical scars. My dad was thrown through the window and was also burned very badly. I've been told that we were not found for several hours.

We were taken to the hospital, where I woke up with a concussion. When I opened my eyes, I experienced a moment I've never forgotten. A priest was standing over my bed. He said, "I don't know how to tell you this, but your mom is dead." Then, he gave me a beautiful, carved wooden angel that spun around and played music, and said, "Your mom will always be an angel looking out for you." I took those words to heart. Throughout my life, I have believed that my mom has always been there for me, an angel at my side. I still have that German music box today.

My brother, sister and I came home without our mother and without our dad, who had to stay in the hospital for several months. My mom's younger brother, still in his twenties, and his new bride cared for us. We had very little time to adjust to our new situation, and after all, when you're ten years old, you don't really understand what's happening. Also, times were different then. People didn't know about therapy. I didn't know I had gone through a traumatic experience. I just knew that as the eldest child, I had to grow up quickly.

When my dad came home, I took on adult responsibilities. I planned and cooked our meals and made sure that chores were completed on the weekend. Taking on so much responsibility at a young age, I developed certain beliefs and skill sets that have lasted my entire life. More than anything else, I learned not to be afraid to take chances. In business, I take lots of risks, and this stems from my childhood. For example: when I was eleven years old, I traveled by myself by bus and train to see friends on the Jersey shore, and while I was there, I swam out way past the deep end of the ocean where we were not supposed to swim. My dad worked late, and there was no one home to check to see if I did my homework or not. This early independence taught me that I could accomplish most anything I wanted as long as I wasn't afraid to try.

There is one thing that I have little tolerance for, though, and that's a victim mentality. I suppose I could have thought of myself as a victim. The loss of my mother was so painful and left such a void: I could have felt sorry for myself. But again, at ten years old, you really don't know how to express those feelings. And even if I had had those thoughts, what good would it have done? It would not have helped me move forward. I believe people can go through pain, heal, and then try to discover what they were supposed to learn from the experience.

My mom was only thirty-two years old and perfectly healthy when she died. Having lost her so unexpectedly, I learned that life can change in a moment. I recognized that I only had one life, and that I could never know when that might be taken away. I knew I had to make each moment count.

Something else truly helped shape my beliefs, and that was trust in the kindness of others. In the months and years after my mother's death, I had so many people reach out to help me, just because they were good people. Our neighbors came over with breakfast. My friend's mothers were always there to braid my hair, or help me when I had teenage boyfriend problems. I knew if I had a problem, I could always call them, even at two in the morning. Every one of those wonderful people who were there for me during those years were not there for any personal gain or money, but because they saw someone in need of help. As a result, I grew up with compassion for others. I've always felt it was important to be there for my friends, family and colleagues in their times of need. When I'm asked how they can repay me, I tell them that the best way is to "pay it forward," and do something that will help someone else.

My mother had two sisters. One of them had had some silly argument with my mom before the ski trip. The next time my aunt saw my mom, she was dead. My aunt regretted this argument her whole life. For me, I try never to leave angry with anyone, especially with my family. But also, in the business world, I try not to end a meeting on a negative note; I prefer to resolve any conflicts or misunderstandings before we walk out of the room.

In business, I have had my ups and downs, but I have learned to persevere, and I appreciate that I've had the help of great people. I don't forget the help I've received, whether from my childhood friends and their moms; teachers who invited my brother, sister and me to their homes for weekends; business mentors and associates who worked with and stuck with me during my early years; or my current colleagues and employees at Prudential Douglas Elliman.

Today, the people who work in my company are part of a family... maybe sometimes a dysfunctional family, but a family. I consider each person—the mail room staff, administrative assistants, the creative group, agents, brokers, and managers—to be part of a team working together to build success.

Sometimes, I wonder what my life would be like if my mom had lived through the accident. I remember watching an old movie about three letters that got lost in the mail. I think about how different the outcome of the characters' lives would have been if they had only received those letters, and about how different my life would be if my mother were alive today. My future was shaped by that loss. I learned how to survive and to do things on my own. I learned to be tough when I had to be, but also to value relationships. And I learned to take care of myself and my family.

At times, I think I have lived a Cinderella story, with all the good and bad. But ever since that priest gave me a carved wooden angel and told me, "Your mom will always be an angel looking out for you," I have felt safe and certain that my mom has been with me, and that she will be with me forever.

A-A-A: Map the Moment

What was the moment of *Awareness*?

_____

_____

_____

_____

What was the moment of *Acknowledgment*?

_____

_____

_____

What was the *Action* taken?

_____

_____

_____

_____

7.

Chances Are

Singer Johnny Mathis performed one of my favorite songs, "Chances Are." I love the title: chance offers so many possibilities and promises, and so much can depend on it. Will you decide to make a left turn instead of a right turn, and have your career suddenly turn around? Will you take the subway, end up getting lost, and meet the love of your life? Will your family be reunited by the turn of a dial? These moments of chance are exactly what happened in the next three stories.

"I followed my heart, and it has been good."

- Bob Kindred

In the music world of soul jazz and the blues, tenor saxophonist Bob Kindred is considered a giant by audiences and fellow artists alike. In America and around the world, his work has been praised by listeners and acclaimed by critics. The National Endowment for the Arts has honored him as well.

I've seen Bob perform several times with his Trio at Café Loupe in New York City, and I play tennis with his wife, Ann Phillips, a most talented jazz singer herself. When I mentioned my book project to Ann, she suggested I speak to Bob about his chance moment. As it turns out, Bob might never have fulfilled his dream of becoming a musician if he hadn't taken one wrong turn onto a particular Philadelphia street...

Jazz Soul

Bob Kindred's Story

Growing up in Pennsylvania, music was a significant part of my early life. I studied the clarinet. I enjoyed playing and I was good at it.

When I was a teenager, my older brother introduced me to a concept known as jazz improvisation. I was fascinated with this technique: it was so different from anything I'd learned before. I started listening to the greats, Benny Goodman and Artie Shaw.

One of my friends had started driving at the age of eleven, helping out with a family gardening business. When we were fourteen, we "borrowed" his family's '53 Buick, and headed off to a famous dance pavilion to listen to Big Band music. This was the first time I'd ever seen an eighteen-piece band, and heard them improvise. The band was Stan Kenton's All Star Band, many of the members of which went on to become quite prominent.

Although I had dreams of a career in music even then, I had assumed my career might be as a clarinetist in a symphony orchestra. That night changed my perspective. At my next clarinet lesson, I asked my teacher how to improvise. He was not receptive, nor were my parents.

I was born into a family of educators. My father was a dean at a major university; a career in jazz seemed a remote possibility to him. In the end, I listened to this academic leaning and continued my study of orchestral clarinet. When I graduated from high school, I was offered a scholarship to Curtis Institute in Philadelphia, a well-known music school. But my family, steeped in academia, thought it would be best if I followed a more traditional liberal arts college path and set my sights on a "real" job.

Discouraged, I followed their guidance. I dedicated myself to this new life, and I decided not to play the clarinet ever again. I simply wiped music out of my mind.

At least, I tried to wipe music out of my mind. I even succeeded for about ten years.

By the time I was twenty-eight, I had a very respectable career as president of my own employment search firm, and business was going very well. But music was starting to creep back into my life. Although I didn't have my instrument anymore, I was listening to other people's music constantly.

Leaving my office one day, I turned the wrong street corner and found myself walking past the Philadelphia Academy of Music. There was a saxophone concert going on. Almost against my will, I stopped in to listen. Hearing that music, I started shaking like a leaf. The sound of it was thrilling.

After the concert ended, I was compelled to go backstage. I introduced myself to the performer, who was none other than Phil Woods, my favorite saxophonist! We spoke for a while, and I heard myself say, "I'd like to study with you."

"Do you play?" he asked me.

"I don't play anything, and I don't have an instrument," I replied.

But apparently, I was convincing in my desire, because Phil agreed to work with me. "If you're serious," he said, "come to my house and bring $500. I'll buy you a sax."

The next morning, I showed up at Phil Woods' home with the money. Again, he tried to talk me out of the lessons, but I knew I had to get back to the music.

For six months, I studied hard, practicing for hours at a time. I was hooked. I hung out at jazz clubs and played with local musicians whenever I could. It felt so incredible to be playing again, like awakening from a dream. I'd been lucky to have had great teachers as a child: my association with music was a happy one, and those memories flooded in. Music literally consumed me.

At this point, I was burning the candle at both ends, running my business during the day and practicing the sax at every other waking hour. Sometimes I would practice in my office all night long, not even going home to sleep. Finally, the super of my building came by to tell me that the night cleaning crew were not getting their work done because they were too busy listening to me play!

So that I could keep up my practice schedule, I rented a studio in a music school. It was a good decision: there, I met other jazz musicians who invited me to jam with them, and who recommended me to groups in town. Meanwhile, my business partners were becoming irritated by what they saw as my changing priorities. When they found out I was trying to secure an audition with the Glen Miller band, they decided I was a business liability, and I agreed. I couldn't concentrate on the business any more: the music was it.

From there on in, music became my life. I was playing constantly, getting more gigs. A real turning point was when I was invited to play in Buffalo with the famous jazz organist Charles Erland. After arriving, I happened to look out the window of my room in the Motel 400 to see the Glen Miller Band's bus parked outside. I couldn't believe my luck: my attempts to get an audition with them only a short time before had led me nowhere. Feeling brave, I ran outside and introduced myself to the band members.

"Why are you in Buffalo?" they asked.

"I'm playing with Charles Erland," I told them.

Apparently that was all they needed to hear. "If you're playing with him," they said, "you don't need to audition with us. When we get an opening, we'll call you."

I did get that call only a few weeks later, and I played with The Glenn Miller Band for close to two years. From there, I went on to play with Woody Herman's Jazz Band. After all my hard work and endless hours of practice, I felt that my true talent was finally being recognized. I was a real jazz musician. Eventually, I settled in New York City, where I continued my association with major jazz musicians, and started recording, touring, and leading my own groups. Today, my band, the Bob Kindred Trio, plays around the world, creating music and CDs for jazz lovers.

When you're playing with great musicians, it's just magical. It's hard to put into words, but for me it's as though I'm outside myself, in a deeper, more spiritual place. I feel so privileged to be doing what I do. My family, once skeptical, now is totally supportive of my career.

Looking back, it's hard to imagine that just one moment—the moment when I turned that street corner in Philadelphia and took a left instead of a right turn—gave me the impetus and opportunity to do what I love. I followed my heart, and it has been good.

A-A-A: Map the Moment

What was the moment of *Awareness*?

_____

_____

_____

_____

What was the moment of *Acknowledgment*?

_____

_____

_____

_____

What was the *Action* taken?

_____

_____

_____

_____

"It has been difficult leaving the ghosts of the orphanage behind, but from the first time I met my brothers and sisters, it's like I always knew them."

- Elena A.

Elena is the niece of Alexandra, an old family friend. The first twelve years of Elena's life were spent in a Greek orphanage, until a Greek-American couple adopted her and brought her to Chicago to be part of their family.

Almost forty years later, in one trans-Atlantic moment, members of her birth family miraculously reappeared. And this meeting might never have happened but for a relative's chance walk through her living room one day.

A Greek Odyssey
Elena's Story

I didn't speak a word of English when I arrived in the United States. Everything was new to me: the language, the food, the clothing. It was very scary. Being in an orphanage for twelve years, you begin to think that maybe it's better to stay there; you develop lots of demons and doubts, and even though you have no one but yourself, at least you can be sure no one will desert you. But in this strange new country, I had a mother and father, a grandmother, aunts, uncles, cousins, and even some extended family in Greece. It was an unbelievable change.

Forty years after my adoption, it was one of these Greek relatives who helped to change my life again. One day in 1997, my cousin Daria, who lives in Athens, walked into her living room and turned on the television set just in time to catch the end of a new television show which had premiered that day. A man and woman were being interviewed, and Daria couldn't believe what the woman had to say.

"If anyone out there knows the whereabouts of our missing sister, Elena, who was living in the United States in Chicago, please contact us."

Daria immediately called my aunt Alexandra, who lived in California. "I was watching television," Daria said, "and a woman came on and asked if anyone knew the whereabouts of Elena. How can this be, all these years later? We thought Elena had no family in Greece but us."

At this point, I was fifty years old and married with two children. We had left Chicago and were living in California. Both of my adopted parents had died within one year of each other in the early 1980s, leaving me somewhat of an orphan again, but all of my cousins, aunts and uncles offered great support.

My mother's sister, Alexandra, was called upon to deliver this new news to me. After she told me about this Greek family who were searching for me, she asked what I wanted to do. At first, I wanted nothing to do with them. I didn't want to see anyone who had left me on a doorstep as an infant, which is what I'd been told at the orphanage. As a grown woman, I thought I had put all the ghosts of the orphanage away, but those few days after my aunt's call brought all the demons back. Still after a few days I decided that I should meet with these people.

For some, life begins at forty. My life started all over again, with a whole new family, at fifty. Two days after I agreed to talk with them, the brother and sister from Greece flew to California to meet me. I was so nervous beforehand, but, strange as it may sound, the minute I saw them I felt as if we belonged together.

I have a video of that day. It's amazing. We were all sitting on the couch together, and there was just this bond between us. I had so many questions—but mostly, I wanted to know how they could be sure I was their sister, after all these years. How could this be?

As we talked, all the missing pieces of the puzzle of my childhood came together. They told me that when I was born, my birth mother became very ill and was not able to care for me. She had other small children at home and was told that her newborn could stay at a special nursing home, an orphanage which also acted as a day care center. There, I would be cared for until my mother recovered from her illness. My family paid for my care, and my father went to see me every weekend. A few months later, my mother was feeling better and went to pick me up. When she arrived, she was given terrible news: her baby, Elena, had died.

In her soul, my mother never believed that to be so. She spent years searching, and was never able to find me, but she didn't give up hope. Before she died, she called her children to her and begged them to keep looking for their missing sister. She told them, "I dream of her with outstretched arms saying, I'm still alive, I'm still alive! When you find her, give her this gold cross that I saved for her. My mother gave it to me."

My birth sisters and brother knew very little about me, only my name and the name of the foundling home where I'd been taken. After several more years of searching, and a few changes to Greek law which loosened restrictions on records, they were finally able to uncover more information, some of which turned out to be disturbing. Apparently, I was one of many Greek babies stolen and sold to adoption agencies around the world during the 1950s and early 1960s. Secretly taken from the nursing home where my parents had placed me, I was moved to an orphanage and given false papers which said my mother had died in childbirth. Twelve years later, I was adopted by my family in the United States.

My brother and sisters in Greece had been able to discover the last name of my adopted family, and their address in Chicago, but there they lost the trail again, since my family had left the area and moved to California years before. Since that move, both of my adopted parents had died, and I was married with a new last name.

Discouraged, but determined to honor our mother's dying wish, my brother and sisters decided to go on that Athens television show and share their story. Their decision, along with the twist of fate which put my cousin in front of her television set at exactly the right moment, changed my entire life, and reunited my birth family after fifty years.

I'm still in awe over what happened to me. I grew up a lonely child in a Greek orphanage. Once I was adopted, I became an only child. I love my American family dearly, but it's incredible to know that I have sisters and a brother in Greece!

The summer after my brother and sister came to California, my husband and children and I flew to Greece to meet the rest of my siblings. Unfortunately, my birth father died when I was still a child in Greece, so I never had a chance to meet him, but the rest of my birth family have been incredibly welcoming. It has been difficult to leave the ghosts of the orphanage behind, but from the first time I met my brother and sisters it's been as if I've always known them. We speak on the phone every other week, and visit for two months each summer.

Everything just seems to fit now. I know my birth history, I have family in America and Greece, and I have the gold cross my birth mother saved for me. There is comfort in knowing that, although I never knew her, my mother never stopped loving me.

A-A-A: Map the Moment

What was the moment of *Awareness*?

_____

_____

_____

_____

What was the moment of *Acknowledgment*?

_____

_____

_____

_____

What was the *Action* taken?

_____

_____

_____

_____

"Sometimes in life, you seem to be traveling in one direction, and then an experience changes all that. You end up headed from here to over there, not really knowing how it happened."

- Carl Rosenberg

Carl Rosenberg grew up a "Jersey Boy," and a "Jersey Boy" he expected to stay. He never dreamed his personal and professional life would take him not only out of New Jersey but across the country and around the world.

For months, Carl and I would pass each other in the hallways of the studio where we both worked, never saying more than hello and goodbye. That changed one day: Carl was waiting for a client and sat down next to my desk. Our conversation turned to his moment, a chance encounter on a subway platform in Sweden. After that one train ride, his life was never the same.

128

The Woman on the Bench
Carl Rosenberg's Story

Sometimes in life, you seem to be traveling in one direction, and then an experience changes all that. You end up headed from here to over there, not really knowing how it happened.

That's exactly what happened to me a little over twenty years ago. I'd been managing a talented twelve-year-old singer who'd just won the national Star Search TV competition. My hours were not my own. I had no time for anything that wasn't moving my client's career forward. Between the phone calls, meetings, performances and auditions—plus routine flights from my home in Los Angeles to business meetings in New York—sleep was a memory.

At four o'clock one sleepless morning, I turned on the television. The station was airing a travelogue describing Europe in the fall. I knew I needed a break: the last few months had been physically and emotionally draining. But it wasn't until that moment that I said, "That's it! I'm leaving tomorrow!"

"Where will you go?" my roommate asked me when I told him my plan. I hadn't even thought about a final destination; I just knew I had to get away. I decided that it was a toss-up between Italy or Scandinavia, where I had a friend from college days.

Three days later, I was at my parents' house in New Jersey, going through every drawer and notebook where I might have stashed a list of old phone numbers. I couldn't find my friend's contact information in Sweden, so I decided to go to the Italian tourism office to get the necessary travel information. Maybe it was just because I was so tired, but the representative seemed completely unhelpful, even rude. I was so put off that I dumped the materials he'd given me in the trash as I left the building.

I went to the Scandinavian tourism offices next. The first thing I saw when I walked in was a giant, sun-filled poster hanging on the wall. It seemed to be welcoming me, and I thought, "This is what I need, sunshine and warmth." My mind made up, I headed back home to renew my search for my friend's phone number.

While I was out, my younger sister had come by our parents' house, and she was also looking for something. It looked like she'd assaulted all the drawers: papers were all mixed up, and everything was out of place. But when I opened that first drawer, there was the book I'd been looking for all along.

Over a decade had passed since I'd spoken with my friend Lena, and I wasn't sure if the number was even valid anymore. But I called it, and Lena's daughter answered the phone. The last time I'd spoken to this girl, she'd been four years old. Now, she was a charming, poised teenager. Hearing her voice really brought home how much time had gone by, and how much I'd missed by working the way I did.

Lena got on the phone then, and I asked her if I could stay with her for a while. She said I could, and I boarded a plane the next day. My much-needed vacation had begun.

While in the dining car on the train to Stockholm, I became friends with another traveler, a photographer named Guy. We passed the time exchanging Monty Python jokes. I could already feel myself starting to relax. When we arrived in Stockholm, Guy invited me to meet him at an English pub in town one evening that week.

But no sooner did I arrive at Lena's beautiful lakeside cottage than I came down with a miserable cold. I spent the next week nursing myself back to health, staring out of the guest cottage window at the raindrops hitting the water. Finally, by the end of the week, I was well enough to call Guy. We arranged to meet at the Tudor Arms in Stockholm, and I took the train into the city.

After my evening out, I headed back to the subway platform, still feeling a bit sick and disoriented—after all, I'd hardly been out of the house in ten days. It was late, and I was the only one on the platform; there was not another soul in sight. When the next train arrived, it was packed with people, and I had a hard time squeezing myself into the car. Just as we were about to leave the station, I looked up at the destination information above and realized I was on the wrong train. In my mental fog, I hadn't even looked before I'd stepped on! Shoving my way through the crowd, I jumped back to the platform just as the doors slammed shut.

Before the train had arrived, I'd been alone on the platform. But in the mere moments it took me to get on and off that train car, a stunning woman had taken a seat on the bench behind me. It was as though she'd appeared out of thin air.

As I looked at that beautiful blonde Scandinavian woman, I had a sense that a window had opened in my life, and that another one had closed right in front of me. It was the only time in my life I'd ever had that sensation, and I haven't felt it again since. But I knew at that moment that a chapter of my life was ending, and another just beginning.

Since I had no real idea where I was going—after all, I'd almost gotten on the wrong train—I asked her for directions. As it turned out, she was headed to the same suburban town I was. Her father had just passed away, and she was going to be with her mother, who lived not a mile from Lena near the lake. During the twenty-minute train ride we shared, we talked easily. Her name was Birgitta. Her father's name had been Carl, like mine.

When we parted ways, Birgitta gave me her phone number and invited me to a party she was hosting at her apartment in Stockholm in a few days. I accepted, of course: I was already looking forward to seeing her again.

But I had trouble reaching her. Whenever I called the house, Birgitta wasn't home. Her mother always answered the phone, and since she didn't speak any English at all, I couldn't even leave my phone number or a message. Still, I thought Birgitta should have gotten in touch with me, and when I didn't hear from her I was angry.

Lena suggested that I keep calling. Our meeting on that train platform, Lena said, was too perfect, like a scene from a movie. It had to mean something. I followed my friend's advice, and although I did miss the party I eventually managed to reach this mystery woman. The two of us went dancing in Stockholm soon after, and she showed me some of the sights of the city. I was smitten. I wanted to spend as much time with her as I could.

When we had dinner the following weekend, Birgitta mentioned that she was headed to New York the following Thursday for a screening of a film she'd appeared in. Although I hadn't booked a return ticket to the States yet, my immediate reaction was to say, "What a coincidence! I'm supposed to be back in New York next week too." We agreed to meet in the city for dinner.

At that point, I knew three things. One, I simply had to get back to New York before she arrived. Two, I had to be the one to meet her at the airport. Three, my infatuation with her bordered on obsession, but it drove me. After calling every airline, I was told that the only way to get back to the States in time would be to head for London and try to fly standby that Thursday morning. So that's what I did.

Back in New York, I waited for Birgitta in the terminal. People were disembarking from several planes, and the terminal was packed. I thought I was too late, that I had missed her, or that I would miss her in the crowd—but then, there she was, walking straight toward me along the velvet-roped corridor. She waved when she saw me, but then her expression changed. I looked to my right and saw that someone else was waiting for her too. "This must be the man who had sent her the plane ticket," I thought. He started walking toward her; Birgitta looked at me, so I threw my hands up in the air to let her know I wouldn't approach.

I watched as this other man reached her, and as they talked, he looked over at me and back to her. I stayed where I was, stopped cold in my tracks. Was this man her boyfriend? Had I come all this way for nothing? But apparently, I'd gotten the wrong impression, because the next thing I knew the three of us were sharing a cab into the city. We dropped Birgitta's associate off at his hotel and the two of us headed to the Jersey Shore to have dinner with my best friend, just like we'd planned while we were still in Stockholm. When we arrived to find my friend and a bottle of Grand Marnier waiting for us, I knew that all my efforts had been worth it.

Birgitta and I have been together for twenty three years. We have a twenty-one-year old son who, like me, is interested in music. As a producer and executive, my work takes me around the world. We split our lives between New York, Los Angeles, and Stockholm. I still work long hours, but my job isn't my whole life anymore.

I think often of that moment on the train platform in Sweden, and how it shifted the course of my whole life. What would my life be like now, if I hadn't seen that travelogue on television at four o'clock in the morning? If I'd gone to Italy instead of to Lena's house in Sweden? If I'd stayed on that crowded train—the wrong train—instead of jumping off onto the platform at the last minute only to see this beautiful woman sitting on the bench? How different would my life have been, if I hadn't gotten off to meet her?

I don't know the answers to those questions, and I never will. All I can say is that I'm glad I did all of those things, because that amazing moment on the platform led to love, a life shared, and a wonderful son.

A-A-A: Map the Moment

What was the moment of *Awareness*?

_____

_____

_____

_____

What was the moment of *Acknowledgment*?

_____

_____

_____

_____

What was the *Action* taken?

_____

_____

_____

_____

8.

Accidents of Change

In three different ways, I was introduced to three men who had serious life decisions to make. Their choices, made after terrifying moments, now inspire so many others.

"I realize that I am not my body. I'm a man and I'm alive."

- Jim MacLaren

I attended a business seminar and sat next to a young entrepreneur from Canada, Orly Reitkopp. At lunch, a group of attendees went out to grab a quick bite, and we spoke about our current projects. I, of course, mentioned the book I was writing, and Orly told me about an amazing man named Jim MacLaren, whom she'd recently met.

Jim is a motivational speaker who describes life as "a journey," a process in which we learn about ourselves and how to deal with challenges. Seated in his wheelchair, Jim shows us all by example how to "choose life to the fullest, without excuses, without regret." Even after two life-changing accidents, numerous medical challenges, and the loss of a promising sports career, his personal strength and desire to lead the most fulfilling life possible are contagious. His moment—actually moments—will inspire you.

Choosing Life

Jim MacLaren's Story

When I was a young boy, my family moved a lot. My parents divorced when I was eight years old, and as the eldest child I felt a responsibility to act as head of the household. I helped with chores, cooked meals, and looked after my siblings. Sports were my outlet, and soon became my life. It didn't matter which sport; I loved them all. Finally, though, I gravitated to lacrosse and football, maybe because of my size: I stood six feet two inches tall and weighed three hundred pounds.

After graduating from high school, I was fortunate enough to be accepted at Yale University, where I played defensive end for the Bull Dogs. My family was not wealthy, and to meet expenses I needed scholarships. I also had to work forty to fifty hours a week. At that time, I hoped to play football professionally, or perhaps become a lawyer.

I also enjoyed acting, and decided to study theatre at Circle In The Square in New York City during my summer break. My girlfriend had already moved to New York, and I got a job working as a bouncer at a nightclub.

I was twenty-two years old, and about to have my first life-changing experience.

It was one of those perfect, crisp, October fall days. I'll never forget the air, so full of possibility. I was leaving an interview for a bartending job at an Italian restaurant, and looking forward to a scene study rehearsal that evening for a David Mamet play, *Glengarry Glen Ross*. I got on my motorcycle and took off down the street.

I remember driving down Fifth Avenue, appreciating the fancy shops and the unusual lack of commercial traffic that day, thinking that one day I would have enough money to shop in those stores. I noticed the 42nd Street library. And that's the last thing I remember before I blacked out.

What happened has been told to me. A bus went through the red light at the intersection of 34th Street and Fifth Avenue. It struck me and threw me eighty-nine feet. Two women who had just attended a prayer meeting called for help, then knelt by my body and prayed for me. They stayed close by until the paramedics arrived and transported me to the hospital. I've been told I was thought to be dead on arrival.

The first eighteen hours were spent trying to save my life. I had a ruptured lung and spleen, and was in a coma for six or seven days before my condition became stable enough to amputate my left leg below the knee.

Then, my healing began.

I was transferred to a wonderful rehab center in New Jersey, where I spent months learning how to walk with my prosthetic leg. Finally able to return to some semblance of "normal" life, I went back to Yale to complete my studies. The hallways seemed so much longer now: I'd been a three hundred pound defensive end, but now I hardly had the strength to get up from my desk and walk down the hall to my next class. But I managed to complete my course work, and was accepted into the graduate program at Yale.

It was suggested that swimming would be good rehab for me, so I decided to try it. At first, I was embarrassed to take off my prosthetic:

with only one leg, I felt like a rock with arms. But I took swimming very seriously, and soon I started losing weight. That first year, I lost 120 pounds. I also discovered that it was easier for me to ride a bicycle than to walk, since bicycling took the pressure off my stump. I thought, "Let's see how many miles I can ride." Soon, I'd built up my stamina enough to ride for ten miles.

My early passion for sports helped me a lot. While I wasn't able to play football any longer, I was swimming and biking long distances, and eventually I decided to enter a triathlon. I knew I could now swim and bike, even walk, but I had never tried to run with my prosthetic, so I started training, hopping and skipping to get the feel of running.

The first races I participated in included swimming for one mile, biking for twenty-five miles and running for 6.2 miles. Before the accident, I had participated in team sports like lacrosse and football, with coaches and teammates for support, and with opposing players to compete against. Now, I was competing against myself.

Before one race, I trained so hard that my girlfriend had to help me bandage my bloodied leg. But I was determined to run the race. Adrenalin got me through the first few miles: I felt great, and I couldn't get over the beautiful scenery I was passing. At one point a school of ducks swam out of a large pond, spread their wings, and in formation flew overhead. Hopping, skipping and walking for that portion, I finished in last place at one hour and three minutes, but with the police cars and the cheering crowd waiting at the finish I still felt that I had won. Then, I got on my bike, and soon overtook some of the other contenders. As I rode, I remembered being eight years old, playing outside my house, and thinking "I'm supposed to do more with my life."

After that race, I trained more and lost even more weight. One month later, I ran the Boston Marathon and became the first amputee to finish in less than three and a half hours, but it wasn't enough. I wanted to push myself even harder. I started thinking about an Iron Man competition, a race for distance. Soon, I was officially training for this event, which is like a triathlon on a larger scale: a 2.4 mile swim, 112 mile bike ride and 26.2 marathon run. I traveled to remote areas in Canada and Hawaii to compete. By 1992, my personal best was ten hours and forty-two minutes, a world record which I held for twelve years.

That was a busy time in my life: I was enrolled in grad school, participating in marathon and triathlon competitions, and had been hired as an actor, playing a physical therapist on a soap opera for one year. A sports manager saw how much I was doing and asked me to draft a few thoughts to share with other athletes. When I sat down to write, more than twenty pages flowed out of me, and I knew I'd found a new creative outlet.

After that, in addition to grad school, acting, and racing, I added speaking engagements. I spoke about the gift of being alive, and recognized that while each of us have confinements that define us, those confinements cannot limit our human potential or dampen our invincible spirit. When one door shuts, thousands of other doors open.

And my life was about to change again.

It was June of 1993 and I had a race coming up in California. I was living in Colorado at the time, and on the day before I was scheduled to leave I sat on my back porch to read a spiritual book. The sun was very bright that day, the Rocky Mountains were breathtaking, and the children riding bicycles on the street reminded me of myself as a child. I reflected on the eight years that had passed since losing my leg. I had come to terms with what had happened, and I appreciated the gift of my life. Tears flowed, and when my girlfriend asked me what was wrong I said, "Something amazing is about to happen."

I flew to California the next morning, and began the race. I completed the swim. And then, during the bicycle portion, one of the traffic marshals allowed a van to enter our route. The van plowed into me and I went head-first into a signpost.

My premonition that something amazing was about to happen had come true, but not in the way I'd imagined. I was diagnosed with a broken neck, and within an hour the doctor announced that I would never again be able to move from the chest down. I wouldn't be able to walk, only shrug my shoulders and move my biceps. I was a paraplegic.

I remember thinking, "I don't know if I can do this a second time around." During my rehab in Denver, there were many complications, several surgeries, long periods in the ICU, pneumonia, and blood clots in my leg. But the first time I laughed, I thought, "I may not be able to walk, but I'm still able to laugh!" I looked outside, and the sun still shone. The landscape was still beautiful. Even though I would need help for the rest of my life, life was going to be worth living. Laughing had actually helped change my attitude.

It wasn't easy, though. After two years of rehab, I thought, "now what?" I had hit rock bottom and knew I had to climb out of the hole. I had to take action. I could have given up, but I chose life.

In 2005, I started the Choose Living Foundation to help others engage in life and develop their human potential no matter their circumstance. I was also fortunate enough to be the recipient of the Arthur Ashe Courage Award at the 2005 ESPY Awards. At that ceremony, I was honored to share the stage with Emmanuel

Ofosu Yeboah from Ghana, who was born disabled. In my public speaking, I'd been talking about "engaging life"—but when Oprah Winfrey introduced Emmanuel and used the phrase "choosing life," something stirred inside me. I remembered again my eight-year-old self, playing outside my house, knowing that there was more to life, that something bigger was going to happen. My two accidents had stripped my ego: I'd been a burly football player, and now I was confined to a chair, but I could still choose to live. I could still choose to help others, and continue to speak about human potential. I'm grateful to Oprah Winfrey for her thoughts, because they renewed my courage.

Though I wake up each day in pain, and sometimes it's hard just to get out of bed, I know that my life is going to be worth living. Though I may be confined to a wheelchair, we're all confined in some way, and my emotions and my intellect are still free. I have completed two Master's degrees, and I'm working toward a Ph.D. I realize that I am not my body: I'm a man, and I am alive.

A second-grader once asked me, "How do you know when you're living the right way?" I answered, "When you're living with compassion, love and integrity." Reflecting back on that answer, I now add, "Try to focus on something that made you feel good, and think back on that *moment* to help you reconnect with life."

People ask me what it's like to inspire others, but I don't think of what I do that way. I look at the word "inspire," and think that it means "breathing in spirit." Your life can change in a single moment. Mine certainly did—twice, in fact—but my spirit is still strong. Your moment of change might be more subtle, and you might not recognize it until years after it happens, but once you do, you change your intention, and therefore change your life. I hope that you, too, can chose to live life to the fullest, without excuses, without regret.

A-A-A: Map the Moment

What was the moment of *Awareness*?

_____

_____

_____

_____

What was the moment of *Acknowledgment*?

_____

_____

_____

_____

What was the *Action* taken?

_____

_____

_____

_____

I had a feeling of "Oh, no! I'm not ready to go!" I had so many questions: Had I lived fully? Had I ever really loved? Had I mattered?"

- Brendon Burchard

While attending a Mark Victor Hansen Mega Book Expo, I heard one of the invited speakers share his personal and professional life story. The audience was engrossed in what he had to say. Soon after, I contacted that presenter, Brendon Burchard.

Brendon is the author of the best-selling book, *Life's Golden Ticket*. He's also a leadership speaker and management consultant. With multiple clients from Fortune 500 companies, startup businesses, non-profit organizations and universities, his career is thriving. He's highly sought-after as a guest on television and radio shows, and his seminars across the country reach thousands of people. He is the very definition of success—but that was not always the case.

Brendon's story, and the way in which he handled his moment, could change the way you look at your own life.

Second Chances

Brendon Burchard's Story

Growing up in Great Falls, Montana, I was totally average. Nothing really distinguished me from anyone else. When I look back at myself as a teenager, I see a cocky and self-interested young man, driven by the need for recognition.

My status changed, however, after a family trip to France. I shared some of the photos I'd taken on my travels with my high school class, and both my art teacher and my journalism teacher were very impressed by my slide show. They told me I had "a great eye," and asked me to join the school newspaper. My creativity bloomed with the help of my teachers, and eventually I became managing editor for the paper. We received several honors, including a nationwide first place for a high school newspaper.

After graduation, I went on to study journalism at the University of Montana. Life was good. But change was just around the corner.

After my first year of college, my relationship with my first real love came to an abrupt end. I was devastated. The experience sent me into a downward spiral of doubt and self-hatred. I began to question everything about myself, including my reasons for being here at all. Depression set in, and I couldn't shake it. I had to get away.

In my search for escape, I took a job with a transportation company in the Dominican Republic. Though I was far away, the distance didn't help. The loss and pain were still there.

One night, I was sitting in the front seat of a colleague's car, headed back from a client's home. It was dark, and the headlights let us know we were maneuvering a winding curve of the road. Suddenly, the car started to shimmy from side to side. My colleague grabbed the wheel tightly in both hands, and I had a sense that something terrible was about to happen.

As the road disappeared beneath us, the car radio and everything around me went silent. It was as though time stood still.

When time started again, we had crashed the car somewhere off the highway, and were sealed inside a mass of twisted metal and shattered glass. Somehow, I forced myself out through the jagged remains of the windshield, and found myself standing on the hood of the car. I was in shock, covered in blood, and yet everything was suddenly so clear.

I hadn't noticed it before, but the moon was beautiful that evening—a shining blue moon, extraordinarily large and bright, with rays shooting out in every direction. Clarity and brightness replaced the dread I'd felt since the end of my romance. I believe this moment changed my life forever.

If the circumstances had been even a little different, I could have died that night; I knew that, even as I climbed out of the wreckage. But in that moment of stillness, I didn't see my life pass in front of me. Instead, I felt an anxiety, a feeling of "Oh, no! I'm not ready to go!" I had so many questions: Had I lived fully? Had I ever really loved? Had I mattered? My life had been so empty since the breakup, so focused on the past, on what might have been. But that car wreck connected me to my future and lifted me out of my self-pity. Suddenly I felt an overwhelming sense of awe. I was still here, against the odds, and there must be a reason for it. I had been given an opportunity—a "golden ticket," a second chance at life.

My colleague and I both managed to survive the accident, but I was irrevocably changed. No longer was I driven by a need to impress others, a need to be recognized. Instead, I had a profound sense of gratitude.

I returned home to Montana a different person, and began to reconnect with people. Standing on the hood of that car, I'd thought about who would miss me when I was gone, and who I would miss. I felt I had to tell the people in my life that I cared about them. As a nineteen-year-old college kid, I also began to ask the question: what would I do to live up to the promise of my second chance? I decided that I wanted to help other people achieve their goals, and maybe even help them realize their own second chances.

Back at the University of Montana, I changed my major from Journalism to Political Science and Communications, concentrating on how to create and motivate change. For my Master's thesis, I wrote about student leadership. This became the subject for my first book, *The Student Leadership Guide*, which helps students become leaders in their classrooms and communities. Since most universities have some sort of student leadership program, this became a topic I could address nationally while speaking to groups of students.

For several years after the release of that first book, I acted as a consultant to a major company, addressing topics of leadership and change. In the back of my mind, though, I was continually focused on my second chance, and how I could continue to use it wisely.

During this time, I started to formulate an idea for another book, which I titled *Life's Golden Ticket* since that's what I felt life had given me on the night of the accident. I knew I wanted the story to be a mystery: I had always liked mysteries. I also wanted to include some of the many lessons I'd learned in my years as a consultant. Thinking about the many places one needed a ticket to enter, I decided to set my book in an amusement park.

To begin, I took a piece of paper and drew a line down its center, making two columns. On one side, I listed the lessons I wanted to share. On the other, I listed attractions one might see in an amusement park. Then, I matched them up. For example, I wanted a reader to understand what happens when their life gets stuck and they spin out of control, and bumper cars seemed the perfect vehicles to demonstrate the process. I matched the high wire to the value of taking one step at a time, and decided that the strongmen in the sideshow matched my lessons in how to remain strong through adversity.

From that humble beginning, the book eventually came together in a parable using amusement park rides and circus performers to help the main character figure out his personal mystery. His journey into self-realization, which took him from feeling trapped in the past to seeing the possibilities of the future, paralleled my own growth and transformation. And with the book's completion, the vision I had that night on the hood of a wrecked car had come true: I had used my second chance to help others see their own opportunities. My life mattered because I was helping other people make their lives matter.

Looking back at that accident is not as painful now as it once was. The memory reminds me of what is truly important. I know that the magic of change, and of transformation, can come in mere moments. My own moment caused me to totally change my life's direction. It made me more caring, more understanding and more willing to help others. More than ten years after the fact, I'm in a loving relationship, happy with my life, and grateful every day that I can help others find their own "golden ticket."

A-A-A: Map the Moment

What was the moment of *Awareness*?

_____

_____

_____

_____

What was the moment of *Acknowledgment*?

_____

_____

_____

_____

What was the *Action* taken?

_____

_____

_____

_____

"After my accident, I never thought that I could have a career doing what I love. But with hard work, I believe you can be successful at anything."

- Dennis Walters

Years ago, while I was producing a morning television show, my mother sent me information about her friend's son, an amateur golfer on his way to a promising professional career; she thought he would be an interesting guest. Unfortunately, that show ended, but Dennis Walters had a story to tell and I was so pleased to have an opportunity to include it in my book.

Since the age of eight, Dennis Walters excelled at the game of golf. His youthful skills brought him trophies, titles, college scholarships and a number 11 ranking in the United States Golf Association Amateur Championship. After graduating from North Texas University, his hectic schedule included daily practice, frequent travel, and competition in national and international tournaments. With his ultimate goal of becoming a PGA touring professional constantly in his mind, his passion for golf grew daily. But all that was about to change.

What do you do when your whole life is turned around and flipped over? Dennis is an example of how you can pick yourself up and start all over again, and in the process benefit many people.

A Golfer's Moment

Dennis Walters's Story

Before one major tournament, I decided to spend a relaxing afternoon on the golf course with some buddies. The weather was warm and sunny with only a few clouds hovering over the manicured green lawns. The day seemed perfect. By the time I arrived, my friends were already out on the course, so I got in a golf cart and headed off to meet them.

As I rode down the path, a steep incline covered with gravel and stones, I saw my friends waving to me. I wasn't traveling fast when I started, but with the cart gathering speed on the slope, I put my foot on the brakes to slow down. The brakes failed, and I couldn't stop. I was thrown and landed on the edge of the path. When my friends ran over to help, I was lying on the side of the course unable to move.

I was taken to the hospital, and received the devastating news. There wasn't a scratch on me, but I hadn't escaped injury. I was diagnosed as a T-12 paraplegic, completely paralyzed from the waist down. The doctors said I would never walk again.

I was twenty-four years old, and suddenly I was being told to give up all my dreams of becoming a pro golfer. It was very difficult to accept. I felt more bewildered than anything else, thinking about what had happened to me, trying to reason it out inside. Not an hour went by that I didn't think about the events of that day and what I thought I had lost. One thing I did know: I wasn't going to give up my dream of playing golf. I was going to figure out a way to play golf and make a living, even from my wheelchair.

After five months in hospital rehabilitation, it wasn't easy to adjust to being back at home. I stayed in bed all day and night. Even the simplest things were difficult for me to do now, and I felt defeated. This could have gone on forever, but one morning my father took me down into our basement, where we kept an indoor net for hitting golf balls. Using some cord to hold my chair down, and a strap and pillow to protect me from hitting myself with my club, we devised a way for me to hit golf balls from my wheelchair.

My first attempts were awkward, but my years of daily practice and concentration soon paid off. After a short time, I was able to hit the net with precision, and we decided to test this system outside. It was the middle of winter, but we headed for the front lawn. I was nervous: there were houses all around, and I was afraid I would hurt someone with a flying ball. My first few tries were terrible, but the third one hit the mark. It felt so good to hit the ball again, like I was back in the game.

A friend of mine owned a driving range in Pompano Beach, Florida, and he invited me to visit. After I showed him how I could hit the ball from my chair, we decided to try my system on the course. It didn't work. I had limited movement, and the chair was difficult to maneuver on the greens.

The next morning, I had a surprise waiting for me: a customized golf cart! My friend had redesigned the passenger's side of the cart, replacing the usual seat with a bar stool. When I needed to swing the club, the swivel seat would move away from the cart, giving me room to hit the ball. After each shot, the seat moved back in to become the passenger seat again. This invention became the prototype for my current cart, which swings away 90 degrees.

I had to experiment and modify all of the techniques I'd worked so hard to perfect before my accident. Basically, in trying to overcome my physical limitations, I tried to work on the things I could do and not worry about things I couldn't. The most important thing was that I was playing golf again.

Trying to perfect these new techniques from the chair, I also found a way to putt with one hand while balancing myself on crutches. I mastered sand shots quickly, and before long I was hitting competitive scores. Friends and professionals noticed what I could do in spite of my disability. PGA pros started asking me to conduct clinics at local clubs, to demonstrate ways to play golf while sitting down. I liked putting on the clinics; they made me feel like I was preparing for a tournament again. When I wasn't teaching, I was practicing hard, just like I used to do before.

Today, I perform over one hundred Dennis Walters Golf Shows a year all over the country, combining instructional tips with trick shots—including a 225+ yard drive straight down the middle of the fairway while blindfolded. It never occurred to me that I could make a career of these clinics, but that's exactly what I did. Just like I'd promised myself I would, I'd found a way to make a living by combining my love of golf with my new life in a wheelchair. After my accident, I didn't think I could have a career doing what I love, but I was able to do just that. With hard work, I believe you can be successful at anything. I hope that others, too, can find ways to take what some people might see as disabilities and turn them into strengths.

A-A-A: Map the Moment

What was the moment of *Awareness*?

_____

_____

_____

_____

What was the moment of *Acknowledgment*?

_____

_____

_____

_____

What was the *Action* taken?

_____

_____

_____

_____

9.

Dreams Come True

"Become Your Dream"

- James De La Vega, Artist

"In my life, it might have been easier to back off, but if I hadn't tried, I would have done nothing."

- Bonnie St. John

When I attended a "Getting To Next" dinner hosted by Carole Hyatt, I heard an engaging speaker share a moment I knew I wanted to include in this book. Bonnie St. John is a Rhodes Scholar, Harvard graduate, motivational speaker, consultant, business owner, White House Economic Team member, author, mother, and medal-winning Olympic athlete. She's a remarkable woman and a true inspiration to anyone who has ever faced challenges on his or her personal path to success.

Bonnie has faced many obstacles and has succeeded because she was willing to dream big. Her moments came in the form of a few very special invitations.

Dream Big
Bonnie St. John's Story

My leg was amputated when I was five.

Due to a severe leg deformity, the operation was necessary. I was in and out of the hospital and I experienced a great deal of pain at that early age. Once I had healed enough, I learned to use an artificial leg.

My family was not wealthy. In fact, we were far from it. In school, I not only felt inferior because I had only one leg, but because of my second-hand clothes. I had few friends, and I was often teased by the other children. As a way of coping, I developed a vivid imagination. I spent a lot of time alone, living in a mental landscape of mythology and Nancy Drew. I imagined myself solving crimes, traveling the world and doing great things. I even read on the playground.

When I got older, my social life was limited. I had no dates, but I still had my dreams and my determination to do something exciting with my life.

The first of the invitations which changed my life was offered around my fifteenth birthday. My friend Barbara gave me a gift, a certificate which read:

You are invited for one week of skiing with my family over Christmas break.

I said yes. I didn't even hesitate. Even though I could never run fast, and had been exempt from P.E. throughout my school career, skiing sounded exciting. When I was eight years old, my mother gave me a brochure which pictured an amputee skiing, to show me that I could still do everything that people with two legs could do, and from that brochure I was able to conjure a mental picture of myself on the slopes. Also, I'd seen Ted Kennedy Jr. skiing on television, and he'd lost a leg to cancer. I remembered watching him traveling so fast down the mountain, and I knew I could ski down a mountain too.

Realistic issues soon presented themselves. I had only two months until Christmas: where would I get the money for clothes and equipment? I solved my first dilemma by going to the Salvation Army store, where I picked up a pair of old ski pants; I found a matching jacket at a discount chain store. In my free time, I worked odd jobs to save spending money.

Finding the proper equipment was my second dilemma, and that proved harder to address. I needed special outrigger poles with short tips to give me the balance I needed to ski on one leg. I asked everyone I knew where I could find them, but no one knew. I spent hours researching at the library. I called local ski areas, but all I heard was "no, no information." It was intensely frustrating, and I felt as though each contact led me nowhere. Finally I found a club for amputees. I was so grateful when the president of the club lent me the proper poles.

At last, the time came. Outfitted in my new ski pants and jacket, with my outrigger poles firmly in hand, I was faced with my third and biggest dilemma: how to ski.

My learning experience did not begin well. In fact, it was absolutely horrible. Twenty years ago, lessons were not readily available for the disabled. I had to leave my artificial leg at the bottom of the hill, and when we got off the lift I couldn't even stand up. Never athletic before, I found myself covered in bruises from my continuous falling. My hands were frozen inside my flimsy knit mittens. Once I was actually up on my ski, I had no control, and I couldn't go where I wanted to. It seemed like too big a challenge.

But I tried and rested, tried and rested. I knew what I was attempting was possible, and that if I kept trying I would find enough balance to get down the hill.

Finally, I did it, and I couldn't stop! I crashed into skier after skier. Barbara and her brothers tried to help me, but there was only so much they could do. I was so bad that one of the boys actually had to carry me down the hill on his back! But by the third exhausting day, I could turn left and right, and I could stop without crashing into anyone. In a way, I was lucky: since I had only one leg, my ski tips didn't cross, so I was parallel skiing from the start. Soon, I was able to move up to the intermediate slopes. Despite all my bruises and bumps, I was thrilled. Skiing was as exciting as I'd dreamed it would be.

Many years later, I ran into Barbara's mother. "I'm sorry," she said to me.

"Why?" I wanted to know. "You changed my life when you invited me to go skiing with your family."

"But I tried to talk you out of ever skiing again! You were so bruised. You were bleeding. I couldn't stand seeing that."

I wasn't sorry at all. That experience meant so much to me. It was fun, and in those moments on that mountain I'd been living my dream, doing something exciting.

After that first week with Barbara and her family, I was hooked. I skied whenever I could. Up until that point, I'd never been an athlete: I'd worn therapeutic shoes, had an artificial leg, and got made fun of in school. But now, I was skiing.

As I improved, I started going to ski events for the disabled. I'd always had few friends, but at these events I felt I had friends automatically, people who were like me. I was no longer an outsider with second-hand clothes: I was part of a group, and with each event I was growing physically and emotionally stronger. I started to lift weights, to train my body off the slopes. This didn't just improve my skiing, it built my confidence.

The next step on my journey took place a few years later, with another life-changing invitation. At the age of seventeen, I found a book on ski racing written by Warren Witherell, the headmaster of Burke Mountain Academy in Vermont. Intrigued, I sent away for brochures and applied to the school.

I was thrilled when I was accepted—but the tuition was $8,400, which may as well have been a million dollars. Where would I find that kind of money? I worked tirelessly before that first semester to raise the money, but I couldn't even come close. Heartbroken, I called the headmaster and told him I had failed to come up with the tuition. He said, "Come anyway." I could hardly believe it. He was offering me a scholarship!

I believe that certain breakthrough trajectories can change your life. Faced with that enormous tuition, I could have said, "That's impossible. I can't go to this academy." If I had done that, my life would have gone another way. The same could be said about that invitation to ski with Barbara and her family: I could have said no, and life would have gone on. But at those moments, I chose to say yes. After all, what did I have to lose? I had no fear of failure: most people didn't think much of me anyway. I wore tacky clothes, and I wasn't popular or beautiful or any of the things that mean so much when you're seventeen.

My brother has said of me that the energy I used to catch up to other people is the energy that carried me further. I think this is true. I didn't mire myself in fears or questions. I just kept dreaming big and working hard, because I had nothing to lose if I didn't.

At Burke Mountain Academy, I pushed myself to excel both in skiing and in academics. The first time I competed at the national championships, I did well. While racing and looking for sponsors, I applied to Harvard and majored there in Political Science. Determined to compete in the Paralympics, I took some time off from my studies to train, working as a waitress and as a cashier in gift shops to pay my expenses.

I waited for weeks to find out if I would be moving to Colorado to train for the 1984 Paralympics at Innsbruck, Austria. From across the country, only three amputee women would be chosen for the team. I had trained and competed for three winters and one summer for this one chance. My life had been focused on making the team. If I didn't make it, I'd be devastated.

At last, I received the call, and another life-changing invitation. I made the team and competed that year, winning a Bronze medal in the Slalom and a Silver in the overall competition. At one time in my career, I was the fastest woman in the world on one leg.

At so many times in my life, it might have been easier to back off. Even learning to walk was hard—but if I hadn't tried, I would have done nothing. When I look back to when I received my friend's skiing invitation, when I was offered the scholarship to the skiing academy, or when I was invited to compete in the Olympics, I recognize that my life was irrevocably changed by these moments. I was disconnected, but now I have become connected to the world. In these moments in time, I decided to put it all into action and go for it. Each of them could easily have gone another way if I had said no or didn't try. But I decided to dream big!

A-A-A: Map the Moment

What was the moment of *Awareness*?

_____

_____

_____

_____

What was the moment of *Acknowledgment*?

_____

_____

_____

_____

What was the *Action* taken?

_____

_____

_____

_____

"How is it possible that my dream could come true in one moment?"

- Josephine Rose Roberts

I know I should exercise more, but my routine consists of about ten minutes on the bicycle at the gym. During one of these ten-minute exercise periods, I started talking to the woman on the next bike. Turns out, she had a moment; one which I think will speak to everyone who's ever struggled to reach his or her dream.

Josephine Rose Roberts is a Broadway actress. Her life today is a far cry from that of her early childhood, which was spent in a small town in Ohio. "The big news in town this past year was that Walmart opened up," she jokes.

Josey started dancing at a young age and dreamed of performing, but never expected to have a chance to sing and dance in big Broadway musicals. She did get this opportunity, but like many performers she was faced with frustrations, fears and challenges in the pursuit of her passion.

It was a passage in a highly-regarded book which helped Josey to deal with these challenges, by allowing her to overcome self-doubt and make adjustments to her negative thoughts about her future. With the flash of insight gained in one moment, Josephine Rose Roberts was able to consciously change her attitude and hold on to her dream of performing.

Living A Dream

Josephine Rose Roberts's Story

When I was five or six years old, my favorite thing to do was dance around in our driveway. I had a little children's record player and would sing and dance to the song "We Are Family" over and over.

My parents recognized and supported my interest in dance and signed me up for classes at the single dance studio in town. I loved dancing. I loved the music. I loved everything about the classes. Soon, I was dancing almost every day. I may have been young, but I was very serious, and I learned tremendous discipline from my teacher, who noticed and appreciated my dedication early on and took me under his wing. He insisted on promptness and attendance, but rather than put me off, his strictness and dedication instilled in me a desire to be the best I could be, and helped plant the beginning of a never-give-up attitude.

Although they didn't really understand where my desire to dance had come from, and were anything but "stage parents," my mom and dad were totally supportive of my pursuit. They told me I was special and encouraged me without being pushy. My dad even gave up his free time to act as my personal taxi driver. My parents believed I had a gift and that it was my responsibility to one day give back.

By the time I got to high school, I'd already been fortunate enough to work with some great teachers. In high school, my teachers helped me to progress even further. During this time, I was also introduced to acting lessons.

Even in the midst of all this, I don't think I realized there was such a thing as a career in the arts. I couldn't imagine that there was a whole big world out there beyond my small town, or that someone could actually become a singer, dancer and actor all at the same time, all in one person.

In college, I studied musical theatre, and that was where my challenges began. Up to this point, I'd been encouraged to perform and praised for my skills, but now my professors did not believe in me or my abilities. In fact, they told me to quit. But even though I heard what they were saying, I knew in my heart that they were wrong.

Through all four years of my college career, I wasn't chosen for a single role. I didn't participate in even one play. One semester, a class was offered to acting students to prepare them to audition for the prestigious Utah Shakespeare Festival. I was very excited by the idea of performing Shakespeare, but my professors did not share my optimism. They didn't even let me apply for the class. I was disappointed and hurt, but I wasn't going to give up. I worked with a private tutor and practiced on my own for weeks. When it came time for the audition, I was ready to show I had the talent to win a part.

When the results were posted, I was thrilled: all my hard work had paid off. I'd been cast in the Greenshow, a variety show which plays just before the main Shakespeare performances. I was in the English and Irish shows, performing little dances and songs common to those cultures during Shakespeare's time. I was also offered a part in *My Fair Lady*.

Though I enjoyed my experience at the Utah Shakespeare Festival, all the negative comments from my professors had taken their toll. I had lost my confidence. I was actually starting to believe that I didn't belong in the world of musical theater.

Before graduation, my classmates and I were required to take internships. Since I'd been told I would never make it in the performance arena, I started thinking, "Maybe I won't be a dancer and singer. Maybe I won't be a performer. But I can try choreography." I took an internship for stage directors and choreographers in New York City.

When I started that internship, I'd almost given up on my dream of performing. But one day, I noticed an ad for open auditions for the touring company of the hit musical, *CATS*. I went to the audition and got the part of the black-and-orange mischievous cat, Rumpleteazer! That year, I traveled across the country, and performed in forty-two states. It was, without a doubt, the best year of my life. When I returned to New York, I also managed to get an agent. Things were looking up.

After my success with *CATS*, my college professors apologized to me for their lack of encouragement. But I believe their discouragement and negativity gave me the drive to work even harder at my craft. Instead of being angry, I am thankful to them.

After that performance, I landed several other roles and felt I was on my way. Then, I didn't work for seven months. Nor did I take singing or dancing lessons. The old doubts returned, and I began to question everything about my career decisions. Had my professors been right after all? I knew I had to separate my emotions from the situation; that I had to treat the process of auditions and callbacks as a business and figure out what to do next. After all, the rent still had to be paid.

It was time to resurrect my early dedication and the lesson I'd learned from my first dance teacher: work hard, and never give up. But I felt completely lost. I needed someone or something to point me in the right direction, to show me the way. I knew that I loved performing more than anything else in the world, and that, while I might not be the most talented girl in New York, people must have seen something in me, or else I would never have won the parts I'd won. But even knowing these things, I let myself slip into a spiral of self-pity for months.

It was during this stressful time that a friend recommended a book called *The Art of War*. The text was written more than two thousand years ago by a Chinese philosopher named Sun Tzu, and deals with honorable leadership in battle, and the preparations and tactics which can help a commander win a war. At first, it seemed like an odd suggestion, but then I read something about the book which really resonated with me. It said, "This book is a kick in the butt for artists."

Once I started reading *The Art of War,* I couldn't put it down. I must have read it two or three times in a row, cover to cover. Sun Tzu's words, written more than twenty centuries ago, really were the "kick in the butt" I needed. I had found that "something" I needed to help show me the way.

Toward the middle of the book, Sun Tzu talks about the differences between amateurs and professionals. I clearly wanted to be a professional in my field, and do my job well. But when I read his words, I interpreted them to mean that I was failing my art, and failing myself, because I was no longer learning or developing my craft. I needed to get off the couch, go to dance classes, show up for singing lessons. If I focused myself and made myself available, the book told me, I would open myself to positive changes. I would no longer feel as though I had nothing because I would be doing something.

The moment I read Sun Tzu's words for the first time, my life changed. I decided then and there that my life was supposed to be dedicated to musical theater, and if I kept working and practicing, everything I wanted would come to me. I'd always believed that people who work hard are rewarded, but somehow I'd lost that confidence in my own life. After reading those words, I felt vindicated, and I knew that even though there might be people out there with more talent than me, I could make up the difference with a whole lot of hard work. If I honored the ideas in the book, I believed, I would be performing again.

I'm a little gal from a small town. I don't have conservatory training like many of my fellow actors, and I often feel that I am where I am by the grace of God. I constantly remind myself that I'm on my own journey, and that I have an obligation to stay focused and keep going. Now, I reread *The Art of War* whenever I feel myself getting too lax. Each time I read it, I learn something new, and recommit myself to my professional work ethic and my desire to perform. I never want to stop evolving as an artist.

It's funny, but when I was out of work for those long seven months, I told a friend, "I just want to work. The role doesn't have to be grand. I don't care if I have to play a tree in the background!" That same night, I sat on my fire escape with my journal and wrote a letter to God. "I don't know if I can be here and do what I'm supposed to do," I wrote. "I have doubts and fears."

The very next day I got offered a part in *The Grinch Who Stole Christmas*. I'll never forget the moment I got that phone call: I was shaking. And yes, I was hired to play a dancing tree! I was so excited that I put on shoes from two different pairs, pulled my shirt on backwards and ran down the street grinning and laughing. I was going to be on Broadway! Finally, I was going to be singing, dancing and acting, just as I had always dreamed I would. I remember thinking, "How is it possible that my dream could come true in one moment?"

A-A-A: Map the Moment

What was the moment of *Awareness*?

_____

_____

_____

_____

What was the moment of *Acknowledgment*?

_____

_____

_____

_____

What was the *Action* taken?

_____

_____

_____

_____

"A friend of mine told me that if you have to try very hard to get uphill, it's not right. It should be easier than that."

- Liz Weidhorn

As a young girl, Liz Weidhorn liked putting on shows for her neighborhood friends. She fell in love with Doris Day films, and after watching them would act out each scene for her family. By her sophomore year of high school, she knew what direction her life would take; she dreamed of making acting her life's work.

Liz is the sister-in-law of my niece, Debbie. Throughout the years, I attended many of their acting school performances, and each one was excellent. Everyone knew that Liz had a very promising career ahead of her, but changes were afoot. Her dreams were shattered by historical events, and another passion started seeping in. Soon, a new dream emerged.

Bread, Cookies, Cupcakes...I'm a Baker!
Liz Weidhorn's Story

I auditioned for my high school's theater program during my sophomore year. I took the audition process very seriously. Though I naturally gravitated toward comedy, I chose a serious dramatic reading from *Mississippi Burning*, playing the part of an older woman, and practiced it all summer long. My teachers were impressed by how hard I'd prepared, and accepted me into the program. During my time in that wonderful program, I performed in a variety of plays ranging from dramas like *The Miracle Worker* to comedies and improvisational pieces. I especially enjoyed hearing laughter coming from the audience.

In college, I studied theatre, and auditioned for a two year post graduate program at The New Actor's Workshop in New York City. I felt that I was on track to fulfilling my dream of becoming an actor. After graduation, I was cast in several short films and learned new techniques for performing in front of the camera, which is different than performing on stage. But something was happening to my confidence and desire to act. The happiness and intoxication I had once felt while performing was starting to wane. Rather than concentrating on the work, I worried what people thought of it.

Other things were changing in my life during that time. To help pay my bills after graduation, I'd taken a clerical job in a law firm. My love life was in flux: while in the New Actor's Workshop program, I'd finally realized that my long-time boyfriend had not treated me well, and started dating a young man named Aaron whom I'd met in class. Aaron showed me how wonderful it was to be with someone nice. More than anything, though, I was depressed about my career. Acting, which was what I'd wanted to do for most of my life, didn't seem to fit the bill anymore. I was still performing, but getting on stage was becoming more and more difficult.

At this point, I was still living with my parents in New Jersey. When I was a child, my mom would take me into New York to see ballet and theatre. The city seemed so exciting to me, and I wanted nothing more than to move there. Seeing the film *Rear Window*, with Jimmy Stewart and Grace Kelly, reinforced my dream of becoming a New Yorker, but I still hadn't made that happen.

Aaron and I became more serious about each other, and about a year later we decided to move in together. I would be joining him in his New York City apartment, and my dream of living in the City would finally be realized. I moved into the city on September 10, 2001.

The tragic attack on the World Trade Center on September 11, 2001—my first full day as a New Yorker—changed everything for me. I remember wondering: what was the point of acting, of anything at all, if we were all going to die? I was so upset by the horror of the attack, the agonizing deaths, and the threat of further terrorism, I became almost frozen with fear. Soon, Aaron began talking about moving out of the city.

Growing up in New Jersey, the happiest place in my family's house for me was always the kitchen. My mom is a great cook, and the amazing smells coming from her kitchen always filled me with warmth and comfort. I felt safe there. Although I wasn't conscious of it at the time, in the days following 9/11, I found myself drawn to my own kitchen.

I had never cooked before, and I can't explain it now, but suddenly the only place I wanted to be was in the kitchen. I'd watched my mom make hundreds of delicious meals, and I wanted to try to do the same. So I started cooking for Aaron.

At first, I didn't know what to do; I only knew that I was drawn to the kitchen for comfort. I would sauté garlic and onions in oil to get that wonderful aroma, and then try to think of what to cook with them. Soon, I was copying some of my mom's recipes. Aaron's enthusiasm increased my confidence with every meal I prepared.

In time, I began to notice that my anxiety decreased while I was cooking. Although the city was still in turmoil, some of my own good feelings were starting to return. I went to Barnes & Noble and went crazy buying cookbooks. I was especially drawn to desserts and breads; I have quite a sweet tooth.

Making breads became a personal challenge and a passion. Could I actually do this from scratch? Buying the ingredients, preparing the countertop, going through each step of the age-old bread-making process is fascinating. First, yeast must be poured into water that's exactly the right temperature. Then, sugar is added as "food" for the yeast, and the entire mixture is poured into a bowl of flour and kneaded until smooth. From there, it's pretty much a wishing game. I wondered sometimes if the dough would rise so high that the oven door would pop open and the bread pop out! The satisfaction of removing a perfect loaf from the oven was a pretty big accomplishment for someone who'd never baked before, and served as a distraction from my fear of terrorist threats and my guilt over my dwindling passion for acting.

When my mom was in the kitchen, her cookbooks became her journals. As she prepared each recipe, she'd jot notes in the margins about was going on in her life at the time. I started doing that too. It felt as if my mother was in the kitchen with me.

I made loaves and loaves of bread ... and loved the process. The more I learned, the more I wanted to know. From breads I moved on to cupcakes, which I loved eating as much as I loved baking, and from there to baking and decorating larger cakes. My quest for cooking knowledge became somewhat of an obsession. I bought every type of pan, bowl, and kitchen gadget you could imagine. When Aaron and I married a few years later, we never had to register for kitchen items, because we had them all!

The more time I spent in the kitchen, the more I understood that although I'd spent my life preparing to be an actor, I loved food far more than I loved auditioning. I spent all my free time dreaming about cooking and discovering new recipes.

To showcase my new skills and test my recipes, I decided to throw a dinner party for a few girlfriends from acting school. I spent weeks preparing for the big night, made list after list of ingredients, even spoke with wine experts about choosing the perfect selection to accompany my dishes. When the big day finally came, I spent most of the day in the kitchen, making schedules of what I had to do and what time each dish needed to go into the oven. I wanted to be the perfect hostess, and I tried to account for every last detail.

The evening went off with perfect precision. Dinner included Venetian Ghetto Roast Chicken over Tagliatelle noodles, and Caesar salad. For dessert, I baked chocolate cupcakes and topped them with coffee ice cream. My friends loved the food, and for weeks after I savored the feeling of pride I'd had when presenting each of my dishes, replaying the party over and over in my head. I knew from that point on that I only wanted to be in the kitchen. It was the best feeling.

Although I wasn't auditioning anymore at that point, I was still working at the law firm. After the dinner party, I told everyone at work that I had found my calling. I said I wanted to leave my job and work in a bakery. Shortly after that, Aaron and I moved out of the city.

One day, I opened our local paper to see an ad for an assistant position in an amazing cheese shop in my hometown in New Jersey. This was an opportunity I'd been hoping for: at the cheese shop, I'd have a chance to work with fantastic olive oils, cheeses, and breads. It seemed perfect for me.

I got the job, and I learned more than I ever thought I'd know about cheese! I also learned about fine olive oils which, like wines, have unique tastes, textures and fragrances based on where they're grown and how they're pressed. In short, working at this cheese shop, I was in food heaven.

I continued to attack bread-making with tremendous zeal, and began to experiment with baking in large quantities. At first, it seemed that no one would hire a baker with no formal schooling and no experience, but at last I came across an ad which read, "Wanted: Baker/Cookie Decorator. No Experience Necessary: Will Train."

I scheduled an interview and was given the job. I knew I had a real learning curve ahead of me, but I was ready for it. At this bakery, I learned how to bake cookies—lots and lots of cookies. There was a lot of heavy lifting involved, but the smells coming from the huge ovens were intoxicating, and the kneading of the dough was meditative for me. To see flour and eggs and sugar and milk transformed into beautiful baked goods in my hands gave me a feeling of true accomplishment. My favorite smell was the brown sugar dough, which reminded me of gingerbread cookies. Even though I had to get up at 5:00 a.m. and drive nearly an hour to work, I thanked God every day for this job. I wasn't living in fear anymore, because I had found my true calling, and my true happiness.

The tragic events of September 11, 2001 changed my life and pushed me into a new career. Until I sought comfort in the kitchen, I never realized that I had a passion for cooking and baking. A friend of mine once told me that if you have to try very hard to get uphill, it's not right. Acting felt like an uphill battle, but cooking feels effortless to me. I even love the cleanup, because it's a part of the process.

More than anything, I'm joyful and realize that I have a constant smile on my face, even while standing in front of the big mixer swooping out cookie dough. I love telling people that I'm a baker. I'm defined by what I do, and my heart is in it. Someday, Aaron and I hope to open our own gourmet shop, where we'll sell breads, wine, and cheese... and cookies and cupcakes, too!

A-A-A: Map the Moment

What was the moment of *Awareness*?

_____

_____

_____

What was the moment of *Acknowledgment*?

_____

_____

_____

What was the *Action* taken?

_____

_____

_____

_____

10.

Helping Hands

Two Men, Two Lives With Purpose.

"I didn't know what I would do, but I knew I had to do something."

- Dick Young

Dick Young's career as a film and television producer/director has spanned four decades. Over the years, he has been awarded many honors, including three Academy Award nominations for his documentaries and a National Emmy Award for cinematography. Many of his sponsored projects for large multi-national corporations have been produced in his signature documentary style.

In the last few years, the majority of Dick's work has been in producing humanitarian film and video projects for non-profit organizations. While working on one of these films, Dick met a group of people whose plight gave him a purpose that would change the shape of his career and his life.

One morning, I happened to walk by Dick Young's edit session while he was supervising and producing a video project. The visuals and story on the monitor were so compelling that I stood outside the door transfixed. The video project documented lives turned around as rural famers in remote African villages were given a chance at a new livelihood. I interviewed Dick a short time later, and I think his "helping hand" moment will touch your heart.

The Denan Project: A Helping Hand
Dick Young's Story

After I graduated from high school, I had no idea what I wanted to do with my life.

Instead of heading off to college like many of my friends, I ended up serving in the Air Force for three years. There, I was placed in a division that made training films. I went out with various commercial crews, and also volunteered to direct military crews to produce a monthly newsreel seen by everyone in the Air Force. It was on-the-job training for the film industry.

After serving three years, I was able to land a freelance job with *Life Magazine*. Traveling around the world with the *Life* reporters, I was responsible for sound. Every once in a while I would be asked to shoot a newsreel, even though at that point I barely knew the front of a camera from the back. When that happened, I would run to the nearest equipment rental store and ask them to show me how to load and shoot.

Then, I was asked to shoot and edit a film about paper making. Again, I'd been asked to do a job that was totally new to me, a job at which I had no experience whatsoever. I'd never edited anything before, and I had to learn as I went along. Apparently I did okay, because the publisher of *Life Magazine* asked if I would help to put together a film chronicling his career, to accompany the announcement of his retirement. The film was well-received, and I was put under contract with the idea of helping to start a film/

television division where the famous *Life* photographers could work, since we knew the magazine would soon be closing its doors.

Two years later, I decided to strike out on my own. Since then, I've been fortunate enough to make films and videos for major corporations and non-profit entities, including various United Nations organizations, the Ford Foundation, IBM, Exxon, Motorola, Mercedes Benz and the Chrysler Corporation. It's humbling to think that in the past forty years my work has been seen by people in over one hundred countries.

Several years ago, I became involved with charitable organizations that produce films and television shows documenting world humanitarian issues, including poverty, health crises, sanitation issues, and hunger. While traveling on assignment for Heifer International, I learned firsthand of the problems caused by drought and famine in the Horn of Africa.

In the course of that assignment, I decided to take a few days off and do some filming of my own. I thought I might produce a little piece about what I saw. Although there were several areas I could have selected, I chose Denan, Ethiopia. I don't think, looking back, that this was simply by chance.

My crew and I were devastated by what we saw there. Several thousand men, women and children had come to this particular area, hoping to find shelter and fresh water, but there was none. People were sick and dying all around us. They had walked for miles and miles, watching friends and family members die of starvation, dehydration, and illness along the way. For weeks, they'd had barely enough food and water to keep themselves alive.

We were shooting with tears running down our faces. My sound man was sobbing aloud. It was so hard to stand by, just watching and filming, while people suffered in these appalling conditions.

When it was time for us to leave, the district administrator came up to me, and said seven words that changed my life forever. He said: "Please do something to help my people."

I didn't know what I could do, but I knew I had to do something.

I put together a video from the footage, and showed it to various friends. Again, I wasn't sure of the goal: maybe just to raise some money, or hire a doctor for a year. Soon, there were eight of us collecting donations. Sometimes those donations were only $100, sometimes $500. Then, one day, a friend gave us $15,000, and I knew we were on our way.

The eight of us knew that we had to keep our goals reasonable. We couldn't solve the world hunger crisis by ourselves, but we *could* try to offer some medical care to the people of Denan. And that's what we did, opening a two-room facility in an abandoned building.

Now, only a few years later, we're operating a twenty nine room hospital with a paid, caring staff of over thirty people. We have a lab for sophisticated tests, a pre-natal care center, and vaccination and medical outreach programs. We also sponsor agricultural and cottage industry programs, and we're building a water pipeline. Best of all, we have served over forty-five thousand Ethiopians so far, and none of them have had to pay a cent. Thousands of people come to us from across the desert, sometimes walking over a hundred miles with little food and water through areas where there are no roads. The area around Denan is prone to drought and famine, and there are dangerous rebel insurgencies, but at least we have been able to provide a safe haven for those who need medical help.

When I heard the Denan district administrator say, "Please do something to help my people," my life changed. I have a new focus. If I had never heard that plea, I probably would have made a small film about the effects of drought on the displaced people of Ethiopia; maybe I would have taken it to a film festival. But those words, spoken in that moment, were a miracle to me, and they inspired in me a drive to make a difference to the people of Denan and to people around the world. Ever since that moment, my life and future are dedicated to the Denan Project.

A-A-A: Map the Moment

What was the moment of *Awareness*?

_____

_____

_____

_____

What was the moment of *Acknowledgment*?

_____

_____

_____

_____

What was the *Action* taken?

_____

_____

_____

_____

"Following a single line spoken by a great man, I have followed my path."

- Brad Hauter

I attended a NATPE (National Association of Television Programming Executives) Convention in Las Vegas several years ago with Dr. Debi Warner. While walking through the huge convention center, we stopped at one booth that stood out to us with its heartfelt message. I spoke with the producer of the show, Brad Hauter, and discovered that he had a "helping hand" moment to share.

Brad grew up in various areas of the country including Chicago, Indianapolis and Tennessee. No matter where he lived, Brad kept his goal firmly in mind: he wanted to be a professional athlete. In college, he majored in psychology but continued to pursue his passion for sports as a member of the college soccer team. After graduating college, Brad moved to Chicago where, although he remained undrafted, he played professional soccer as a goal-keeper for ten years. This career track might have continued for a long time, but for a single quote read in a book of famous speeches. That quote changed Brad's entire perspective and set him on his life's path.

Listening to the Silence
Brad Hauter's Story

Growing up, my two brothers and I shared a love of sports. If we weren't playing hockey or baseball, it was football, swimming, or cross-country running. We participated in several team leagues and various coaching programs. My parents were very active in our church and outreach programs, and their compassion for others helped me to understand at a very young age how fortunate I was not only to live as I did, but to be able to participate and succeed in sports. It wasn't lost on me that although there were kids out there who were better athletes, I was able to advance because of my parents' support and all the opportunities they provided for me. In high school, many of my friends and former teammates had to get jobs and so couldn't participate in the after-school leagues or summer training camps, but my parents made sure that I could always go, and that I had all the up-to-date equipment I needed to play and compete.

Between high school and college, I happened to buy a book featuring a collection of speeches by the Reverend Martin Luther King, Jr. Since I was always playing sports, I hadn't concentrated much on academics, and I was not a good reader. But this book, *A Testament of Hope*, seemed to call out to me, and as I was flipping through the text a quote literally jumped off the page at me.

The quote was only a single line. It read:

"We as a society should not be bothered by noise made by evil in this world, but rather enraged at the silence of the good."[6]

Dr. King's words affected me deeply. My parents did a lot of mission work through our church: they considered it their purpose. I knew that I, too, had been born with a purpose, but I was only now beginning to wonder what that purpose might be. After reading that quote, I knew that I did not want to remain silent, that I wanted to help others less fortunate than myself. It felt like more than an obligation—it felt like a responsibility.

Still, some time went by before I took action. A few years after I read that quote, I got involved with summer youth camps. I thought that by talking to and listening to young people, I might be able to help them choose a path that would lead away from drugs and drinking, and keep them out of trouble. I also hoped to teach them the importance of making time for others, and expose them to some of the same opportunities my parents had given me. I remember thinking, "I wonder if this might be my purpose."

Looking back, I think at that time my "purpose" may have been driven more by ego than anything else. I thought that as a professional athlete, someone who might be a superstar one day, I could somehow make it happen for those kids. I thought I would give a little time, a little money, and everyone would think I was a nice guy. As I matured, this attitude started to change. I started to realize how hard it was to really make a difference. And I continued to think about that quote; I carried it with me in my wallet, as a reminder.

As a professional soccer player, I only worked six months a year, but those six months involved a lot of traveling. During the remaining months, I worked in our family's sporting goods store with my brothers, and helped run a summer sports camp for young people. Eventually I married, and when my wife became pregnant with twins, I started to wonder how I could be the father I wanted to be when I was traveling six months out of the year. I was proud of my pro career: every year, I had to get out there and prove myself, work hard, and show that I was good enough to be part of the team. Now there was a shift in my focus. It was time for me to be with my family. I couldn't travel with the soccer team anymore.

After I left the team, I continued to work on community projects. One year we took a train to Boston to donate time in a hospice program. On the way home, we spent twenty hours passing through once-thriving steel towns that now stood all but abandoned. Through the windows of the train, we witnessed the severe poverty that difficult times of little revenue had created.

Before this trip, I'd started working with the homeless community in Chicago. Moved by what I'd seen from the train, I decided to start a professional theater group. The actors, all homeless men and women, had an opportunity to see themselves as the subjects of positive news articles and photos, which helped them emotionally, and the ticket sales, which they shared, helped them financially. Watching people who faced so many challenges try to better themselves, I became even more conscious of my role as a father and a husband.

Soon after that, I came across a poster for an organization called Keep America Beautiful, and discovered that they were looking for a spokesperson. Keep America Beautiful is an organization dedicated to improving the environment and creating a more beautiful place to live through education and empowerment. They were launching a new PR campaign to make their efforts more visible, and draw in new volunteers. Since I had already been trying to help people live better and beautify their lives, this seemed like a good fit for me. I called and asked if I could come in for an interview.

The appointment date was set for Martin Luther King Jr.'s birthday, which seemed very significant to me. When I sat down, the interviewer asked me a very pointed question.

"Why are you here?"

"I feel destined to be here," I replied. "I've been guided by a quote from one of Dr. Martin Luther King, Jr.'s speeches for most of my life, and this job will give me an opportunity to live out this mission instead of just saying 'it's a great quote.'"

I got the job, and set to work participating in fund raising and awareness campaigns. After a few years, I was asked to host a morning gardening show in Indianapolis that would address not only lawn care but continue with the message of improving the environment.

From our initial launch on one station, we grew to twelve, then thirty, then over three hundred stations across the country. Our format changed along the way from a lawn and garden show to a home makeover show called *JunkdTV*. On the show, a husband or wife plays a practical joke on their spouse, destroying something around the house which we then show up to fix. While we're there, we do the home makeover, taking the spouse completely by surprise. People who never could have afforded a home makeover can now have a life-changing one.

Our episodes are not extreme makeovers, but all of our makeovers cause extreme results, benefitting and improving people's lives as well as their homes. We visited the Gulf Coast for a project in Biloxi, Mississippi, a city practically demolished by Hurricane Katrina. There, we rebuilt parks and the town green, and within thirty days we saw nine weddings take place on that new grass.

After several years, we launched another television show called *Off the Streets*. Each show chronicles the journies of homeless men and women, and gives them a chance to tell their stories about life on the streets and what it's like to be homeless.

Something changed in me the moment I read Dr. Martin Luther King Jr.'s quote, and that change has continued to drive me throughout my entire lifetime. When I was younger, I wanted nothing more than to be a professional athlete. But when my moment came, I knew that my life would have more purpose than that—and it has. Following a single line spoken by a great man, I have followed my path.

More than anything, I want my children to see my life as an example of a life with purpose, so that they can someday benefit society, and help us all reach a place where the good is not silenced, and the noise of evil no longer bothers us.

A-A-A: Map the Moment

What was the moment of *Awareness*?

_____

_____

_____

_____

What was the moment of *Acknowledgment*?

_____

_____

_____

_____

What was the *Action* taken?

_____

_____

_____

_____

11.

Art and Literature

The following two stories come out of the worlds of art and literature.

"I knew that one day I would have to tell people what I had seen; my art could show the horrors I had witnessed."

- Marc Klionsky

I was taking a real estate course and met a fellow attendee, Motti Levy. At lunch, we swapped career goals and, of course, I mentioned my book. He said he could put me in touch with a gentleman in the arts who had a most special moment. Soon after, I interviewed world-famous artist Marc Klionsky and had an opportunity to meet his lovely wife, Irina. (You'll meet her in Chapter 12.)

Born in Minsk, in the former republic of Belorussia, Marc Klionsky has achieved a noteworthy career and international acclaim in the art world. His works have been displayed in museums around the world, and his soul-wrenching images evoke powerful emotion wherever viewed. Although he started creating art at a young age, it was the Nazi invasion of his hometown that gave his life's work its meaning. His calling was revealed to him, and his creative path influenced, by one moment when he was just fourteen years old.

An Artist's Calling
Marc Klionsky's Story

I was a young boy of six when our neighbor showed me a postcard
from an art museum. I loved it and was fascinated by the pictures.
I wanted to draw the images from that card, and everything around
me. My mother noticed this interest and enrolled me in an art studio
for children, which I attended for several years. Even at that young
age, I felt that art was my true passion.

Everything changed, though, on June 22, 1941, the day the Nazis
invaded the Soviet Union. The Second World War had come to our
border. Minsk was one of the first cities bombed by the Nazis, and
people here hid in their basements for fear of the falling bombs.

On June 25th, my father came home with a major announcement: he
told my mother, my sister, our neighbors in our apartment building
and me that we must leave our homes that very night. My father had
heard terrible stories of the Nazi atrocities in Poland in 1939 and
knew of their attitude toward Jewish people. "The Nazi army will be
in Minsk in a few hours," he said to us. "There is no time. We have
to leave in ten minutes."

We were out of our apartment in even less time than that. For
thirteen days, my family and neighborhood friends tried to stay
ahead of the advancing army. We walked day and night, and people
from other towns joined us as we moved through the woods. By the
end of our journey, our numbers had grown from fifty to almost two
hundred people. Sometimes the German army caught up with us.
Though we tried to hide out in barns along the way, several of our

neighbors were caught. Peeking out of the barns, I was witness to their deaths. I saw them being shot and killed. It was terrifying. The Nazi planes flew very low and when the Germans saw a big crowd fleeing through the woods, they started to shoot or drop bombs. Many people died, but we couldn't stop to bury them. We had to continue on our desperate march.

On the fourteenth day of our journey, we reached a small railroad station. My father somehow managed to get us all on the train, which consisted of empty cattle cars, and we traveled further east. When we finally arrived at our destination, the city of Kazan on the Volga River, we had nothing more than the clothes on our backs. I was only fourteen years old, but as I stood there at that moment, I felt as if I had received a calling. I knew that what I had witnessed while escaping the Nazis would shape my thoughts and future. I knew that one day I would have to tell people what I had seen. I would be an artist and art would tell my story.

Kazan was far away from the battlefront and the bombings. Though my family and I had seen first hand what was happening, the people in our new city could not imagine what the Nazis were doing to our land, and had no idea of the terror we had experienced.

We learned later that after we'd fled our home in Minsk, the Germans had occupied the city. The army had come in, some on motorcycles, and started gunning people down. Most of the Jews were gathered and sent to the Ghetto in Minsk, an area that was once one of the largest ghettos in Europe; the Germans had now sectioned it off to lock in all the Jews.

Adjusting to a new life in wartime was very difficult. It was very cold that first winter even for Kazan, and I didn't have shoes for this weather. My father found a job but it did not provide enough money to feed the family, so I went out looking for a job too. I started working as an apprentice to an artist who did big movie posters. Later, I became his assistant. I also created political posters about the war, telling people through my art about the horrors I had seen. Some of these posters were printed in local newspapers and magazines. Several poets even wrote poetry using images of these posters.

I was able to enroll in school and managed to receive my high school diploma, studying at night because during the day I had to work. Once I graduated, I continued my education, and studied at a drama school for a while.

Two years and only a few speaking parts into my acting career, I overheard the director ask an artist to create costumes for a new production of *Othello*. Immediately, I sprang into action. In an effort to make the costumes historically accurate, I ran to a library to research Shakespeare's *Othello*. Having heard the actors rehearsing the play daily, the images were vivid for me. I went home and drew the required sketches for the costumes.

The next day I showed the theatre director my sketches. He loved them, and decided to make the play's costumes from my work. I now became the theatre artist, designing scenery and costumes for several other plays. I stayed with the drama school for a few more years, sketching and performing a few lines in some plays, but in my heart I knew I wanted to be a fine artist, not just an artist for the theatre. I was grateful, though, for the experience of watching the actors, and listening to the voice of each character they portrayed; this involvement helped my art because it helped me to understand the psychology of people.

In the end, I couldn't ignore my desire to create fine art anymore, so I spoke with the director of the drama school about my wish to study art and asked his advice. He suggested I go to Leningrad once the war was over so I could fulfill my dream.

When the war ended in 1945, I went to live with my relatives in Leningrad and studied at the Academy of Fine Arts. Although education was very important to my family and me, it was not easy for a Jewish person to study at that time. 1949 to 1953 was a difficult time in the Soviet Union, when Jewish writers, theatre people, directors and artists were persecuted, arrested and even killed. In 1952, as a Jew, I was expelled from the Academy, but after Stalin's death a year later, I was allowed to continue my studies. After six years of study at the Academy, I received my diploma and later went on to receive my Ph.D. in Art.

My diploma piece was exhibited at State Tretiakov Gallery in Moscow, and from this image fifty thousand posters were made. My drawings were included in text books for students and sent to various art schools throughout the Soviet Union. I was painting full time and had been named an official Artist of Russia. My paintings were displayed in museums and reproduced in books, magazines and newspapers.

At the beginning of the 1960s, I had a serious health crisis: I had to have surgery for a face tumor. During this trying time, I was once again reminded of my calling. I started to think about what I was doing with my life. Yes, I was painting. Yes, I was the official artist for the USSR. But, I felt that I needed to work for myself. I vowed that if I survived my operation, I would paint only what I wanted, not what the State required. I had to paint what I was feeling, what was in my heart.

I came home from the hospital. With my bandages still on, I started painting from my heart and soul. Now, renewed, no longer restricted to one type of painting, I started to sketch again, this time in charcoal. I was using my art to show my feelings, to show what I believed and how I saw the world. My art was able to show not only my emotions but many of the war images I had witnessed as a teenager.

I had made about ten to fifteen sketches when a friend introduced me to a dealer from England. I was fortunate: the dealer liked what he saw, and suggested I do my sketches as lithographs or etchings. In a few months, I had produced an entire series entitled *Lest People Forget*. My first exhibition abroad in London in 1962 was very successful, as was the next with Marc Chagall. Later, some images from *Lest People Forget* were included in an exhibit sent by the Soviet government to other countries.

In 1974, when opportunity opened that allowed us to leave, my wife Irina, our daughters and I emigrated to the United States. When

An Old Man, Marc Klionsky, 1962
Etchings, *Lest We Forget*

we arrived, I continued to paint what I wanted; now incorporating different styles. With this newfound freedom, I experimented with various techniques I had not been able to use before, and it helped me better express myself. I was fortunate to have some historic figures as subjects for my portrait work: Israeli Prime Minister Golda Meir, Jerusalem Mayor Teddy Kolleck, and Nobel Peace Prize-winning author Elie Wiesel.

Today, I feel that my life is a miracle and that God has been with me always. He saved my life and I was able to fulfill my promise made at one moment when I was fourteen years old. I have not forgotten the horrors of war I witnessed and what I set out to do. Among other works, I made paintings, etchings and sculptures that serve as a reminder. *Lest People Forget* and all my work were made so people do not forget what happened in those terrible years.

Persecuted People, Marc Klionsky, 1962
Etchings, *Lest We Forget*

Lullaby, Marc Klionsky, 1962
Etchings, *Lest We Forget*

A-A-A: Map the Moment

What was the moment of *Awareness*?

_____

_____

_____

_____

What was the moment of *Acknowledgment*?

_____

_____

_____

_____

What was the *Action* taken?

_____

_____

_____

_____

"Reading a poem at the age of seventeen provided me with an idea of the possibilities of poetry."

- Mark Strand

One brisk autumn day, I spent the afternoon apartment hunting with my cousins, Richard Strier and Camille Bennett. They invited an academic colleague to meet us later in the day. Since I had studied the poetry of this accomplished poet, Mark Strand, I confess, I was a little in awe of meeting him—but I did manage to ask the Poet Laureate if he had a moment that he felt changed his life. In fact, he had several.

Mark Strand was born in Canada but spent much of his childhood on the move. His father was a salesman who relocated the family throughout Canada and the United States. As a winner of the Pulitzer Prize for Poetry and former Poet Laureate of the United States, Mark Strand recognizes three specific moments in time that collectively helped shape his future in the arts.

A Poet Remembers

Mark Strand's Moments

The first *moment*:

At the age of twelve, I watched a horror film that is now considered a classic chiller: *Dead of Night*. Combining five different supernatural visions, several directors focus on a group of strangers as they reveal frightening occurrences from the past. Suddenly, I became aware of the strangeness that underlined my own experience. This film stayed with me and prepared me for an interest in surrealism. My own writing became a beneficiary of that interest.

In one of my early poems, *The Tunnel*, the narrator speaks of a frightening figure standing outside his house. Though he tries to chase this man away, he is unsuccessful and decides to escape by digging a tunnel. Here too he is unsuccessful in his escape and emerges to find himself in front of a house, unable to speak.

> *A man has been standing*
> *in front of my house*
> *for days. I peek at him*
> *from the living room*
> *window at night,*
> *unable to sleep,*
> *I shine my flashlight*
> *down on the lawn.*
> *He is always there.*[7]

The second *moment*:

At the age of seventeen, I read the poem *The Love Song of J. Alfred Prufrock* by T.S. Eliot. It was this literary moment that made me want to write poetry. That autumn, I continually read the poem and memorized much of it. It gave shape to many things that I was feeling. Alone in New York City on a work/study program, I somehow, even miraculously, identified with J. Alfred Prufrock. I sensed the necessity of form, of what gives shape to feeling. The poem's measure and rhyme provided me with an idea of the possibilities of poetry.

The third and final *moment*:

I had planned on becoming an artist. I studied literature at Antioch College and then painting at Yale. I didn't decide to start writing poetry seriously until the age of twenty-four when I began reading Wallace Stevens. At that moment, I saw how visual his poems were and thought I could transfer visual images from painting to poetry. Poetry became my art.

Three moments: Viewing a film at the age of twelve gave me a *sense of the surreal* that is found in many of my poems. Reading a poem at the age of seventeen gave me the *possibilities of poetry*. And finally, the writings of Wallace Stevens gave me the *inspiration to write poetry*.

Ideas change over the years. But I'm the same person I was then, except much older. I'm not different; I can feel that person as part of myself. Yet I'm no longer shy, inhibited or unsure. That younger person never knew that he would become what I am now.

A-A-A: Map the Moment

What was the moment of *Awareness*?

_____

_____

_____

_____

What was the moment of *Acknowledgment*?

_____

_____

_____

_____

What was the *Action* taken?

_____

_____

_____

_____

12.

Moments of Meeting

While interviewing actor F. Murray Abraham and artist Marc Klionsky, I learned a little about their personal lives, and about the first time each of these two talented men met their wives. I thought you'd enjoy these *moments of meeting*.

"When you find people who have faith in you, you must hold them dear."

- F. Murray Abraham

Opportunity Knocks
Murray meets Kate

F. Murray Abraham has had several memorable moments in his life. One was the moment when his teacher suggested he take a drama and speech class, a move which propelled him into the world of acting. Another pivotal moment came on the day he met his wife, Kate.

After finishing my interview with F. Murray Abraham, I spoke to Kate and Murray about their first meeting.

"After years of acting in El Paso, Texas," Murray said, "I was finally on my way to Los Angeles to seek fame and fortune. My friend Leonard suggested that when I arrived in California, I should look up a young woman named Kate. I took his advice and called her when I arrived in town.

"After the routine hellos, Kate asked, 'Where are you?' I told her I was downtown.

"'I'll come and get you,' she said. And that's exactly what she did."

"Everything I did that night was counter to my personality," Kate recalled. "I was still in college at the time, living with my grandmother, and was normally quite shy and reserved. Also, I'd just gotten my driver's license, so driving through downtown Los Angeles in traffic was a big deal to me. But I respected the person who'd connected Murray and me, so I wasn't nervous. That day, Murray met a new me! I raced downtown to pick him up, and we hit it off immediately. And when Murray told me he was going to be a star one day, I believed him."

"When you find people that have faith in you," F. Murray said, "you must hold them dear. In all the years of our marriage, Kate has never lost faith in me, and we've never been apart."

F. Murray and Kate have been married for over forty years; they have two children and a beautiful grandchild. They connected because of a single phone call and the action that followed. To me, their story speaks to the need to take chances, to seize moments of opportunity even if you're not clear what that opportunity might be.

A-A-A: Map the Moment

What was the moment of *Awareness?*

_____

_____

_____

_____

What was the moment of *Acknowledgment?*

_____

_____

_____

_____

What was the *Action* taken?

_____

_____

_____

_____

"My only memory was that of the tall, very skinny, scary man dressed all in black, with the long, shiny, dangerous-looking fingernails."

- Irina Klionsky

After interviewing artist Marc Klionsky, I sat and talked with his wife, Irina. As I listened to her speak, I knew I had to share one particular event she mentioned; her first meaningful encounter with Marc. It was a childhood moment she'll never forget.

A Childhood Meeting
Irina Meets Marc

When Marc and I met, we discovered that we both had come from similar backgrounds. Though from different parts of Russia, we both had been forced to leave our hometowns during the Nazi invasion and ended up living in the same city of Kazan.

While talking to Marc about his work in the Kazan Theatre, I told him a story about a moment I had when I was six years old. My mother had taken me to see a play in that very same theatre. It was my first play and I was so excited to see the fairy tale with a real-life princess and prince.

In thinking about that day, I remembered sitting close to the stage, but I had no memory of the prince or princess—or the story for that matter. I couldn't tell Marc the name of the play or what it was about. My only memory was that of the tall, very skinny, scary man dressed all in black with the long, shiny, dangerous-looking fingernails. He frightened me.

When Marc heard this story, years after we had married, he started to laugh, and said, "The man who played that villain was me!"

An unusual first meeting? Maybe…But perhaps fate was trying to cross their paths even then!

A-A-A: Map the Moment

What was the moment of *Awareness*?

_____

_____

_____

_____

What was the moment of *Acknowledgment*?

_____

_____

_____

_____

What was the *Action* taken?

_____

_____

_____

_____

13.

Moments of Being

Following very different paths, the next three people experienced a moment which gave clarity to the rest of their lives. Each person had an *awareness* and/or *acknowledgment* of their moment, and chose a unique *action* to deal with it. One experienced a more cerebral moment, one found her voice, and the third literally stumbled into his lifelong career. Most importantly, each person was able to find his or her moment of being.

"You know you're in the right job when it doesn't feel like a job."

- Robert Knakal

Robert Knakal is a giant in the world of commercial real estate, and he was a dynamic speaker at an Esther Muller educational licensing course. Listening to him, it was clear to me that he loved his job. After decades in the same profession, his passion for work was very real. At one point in his talk, he mentioned that he had started his career in one direction but, because of a simple mistake on his part, his life changed forever. My ears perked up. I knew that I had to find out about the moment that helped him become the person he is today. His moment of being came about totally by accident!

A Career By Chance
Robert Knakal's Story

When I was a freshman at The University of Pennsylvania, I wanted to become an investment banker, like most everyone else enrolled in The Wharton School of Business. During spring break, I submitted my resume to various commercial and investment banks in my area with the hopes of landing a summer position where I could learn about banking, but I didn't receive a single invitation to interview.

Leaving the offices of Payne Webber after dropping off yet another resume, I happened to glance directly across the hall and noticed a sign for Coldwell Banker. Thinking this was another banking institution which I'd somehow missed, I stopped in to inquire as to whether they hired college students for summer work. They said yes, and I handed them my resume.

Later that day, I received a call from their human resources department. They wanted to set up an interview with me the very next day. It was 1980, before everyone had computers, so I went to the library to do research, learn a little about the company, and prepare for my meeting. I was surprised when I discovered that, despite the word "Banker" in the company name, this was not an investment bank but a real estate company.

I thought about not going. But since this was the only company that had actually wanted to schedule an interview, I decided to give it a shot. I was offered a position and I accepted.

From the very first day, I loved working in real estate. The office was filled with young, energetic, hard-working people and I learned a great deal. Although real estate was not a field I would have considered, I discovered that it was perfect for me. For the next two summers, I returned to work there, and after graduation started working with them full time.

Nearly twenty-five years later, I'm the Chairman and Founding Partner of Massey Knakal Realty Services, a full service property company in New York City. I met my business partner over twenty years ago on the very first day I started my career in real estate. When I was a kid, I loved playing Monopoly. Sometimes, a game would last three or four days, and the tension and excitement was thrilling to me. I love working in real estate; I feel like I've been playing a twenty-five-year-long game. You know you're in the right job when it doesn't feel like a job.

I often wonder where I would be today if I hadn't mistaken that real estate office for an investment banking company. That one moment in the hallway changed my career, and my life. Because of it, I became the person I was supposed to be.

A-A-A: Map the Moment

What was the moment of *Awareness*?

_____

_____

_____

_____

What was the moment of *Acknowledgment*?

_____

_____

_____

_____

What was the *Action* taken?

_____

_____

_____

_____

"I was no longer afraid. I began to speak out and reveal my hidden visions."

- Micki Dahne

I was producing a television show, *PM Magazine*, in Miami, Florida when I was assigned to interview psychic/astrologer Micki Dahne. Micki is highly regarded by the Miami Police Department and is often called in to help solve cases where missing children are involved.

I was skeptical at first, but once I got to know this compassionate woman she became the "go-to" person for our show's predictions. Who would win the Super Bowl? Who would be elected President of the United States? Who would walk home with the Academy Award? Year after year, each of her predictions came true: it was uncanny.

Micki and I have remained friends for over twenty-five years. I recently called her to wish her a happy birthday, and she shared with me the moment that changed the direction of her life.

A Psychic Speaks Out
Micki Dahne's Story

As a young girl, I began having premonitions. I was actually able to predict events that hadn't happened yet. But I was too young to understand what it all meant, and so I kept these strange thoughts to myself. In those days, no one understood or mentioned psychics; my mother would punish me for speaking any of my premonitions aloud.

Once I was grown, I married and had three children. I was a dutiful housewife: I cooked, cleaned and hosted lavish dinner parties for my husband's friends and clients.

All that changed in one moment. My husband died, and something began to stir inside me. I became a different person. I not only stopped cooking, I stopped being afraid to speak up about what I saw in my premonitions.

I remember the first time I shared one of these. It was the 1970s, I was out to dinner with friends, and I overheard another conversation at the table behind us. A woman was talking about an upcoming family event; she mentioned her son, whom she'd named for her father who died in the Holocaust. I can't explain what came over me at that moment, but I turned around and told her that her father was not dead—he was living in England!

The woman looked at me in disbelief, but she ended up doing some research, and did indeed discover that the father she thought she had lost was alive and well, living in England. After their reunion, the woman and her father came to visit with me. It was a most humbling and emotional experience.

From that moment on, I continued to speak up whenever that particular feeling came over me. Eventually, I found myself on radio, television and in the newspapers. I've appeared on CourtTV and worked with *The National Enquirer* for twenty-nine years. People now accept my premonitions, and I'm no longer afraid to share them.

A-A-A: Map the Moment

What was the moment of *Awareness*?

_____

_____

_____

What was the moment of *Acknowledgment*?

_____

_____

_____

What was the *Action* taken?

_____

_____

_____

"I somehow knew I was indeed alive and part of the world; I was a being. For the first time, I became aware that I existed."

- Ron Brothers

My friend Gina Rogak introduced me to Ron Brothers several years ago. Ron is a successful marketing consultant living in New York City. His apartment has one of those picture-perfect skyline views and a one-of-a-kind wrap-around balcony—perfect for the dinner parties he enjoys hosting. Filled with tropical greenery, that balcony is a little piece of the country in a city known for stone pavements.

At one of his very tasty parties, sitting outside with the Empire State Building lit up in front of us, Ron told me about a moment from his childhood that has stayed with him throughout his life. He described it as a defining moment, his "moment of being." Perhaps his awareness can help lead you to your own moment of being.

Chasing Butterflies... A Moment of Being
Ron Brothers' Story

At the age of five, I visited my grandparents in Massachusetts. It was a magical time for me. I felt very loved. I was especially close to my grandfather, who would read to me, and with only kind words let me do just about anything. He made me feel special.

My grandfather had both a vegetable garden and a large flower garden. I remember playing outside there one morning; I remember that I was wearing shorts, a T-shirt, and my sneakers as I chased a little white butterfly through the flower garden. My eyes were fixated on this tiny creature flying in front of me. The white of its wings appeared to have a greenish tint as it fluttered all around.

I had been chasing this butterfly for a few minutes when without warning, I felt myself lift out of my body, maybe about three hundred feet in the air, hover, and look down to see that young boy running happily, chasing a butterfly. It was a very powerful feeling for me and I couldn't put it into words back then: at that young age, how do you process a sense of flying and an understanding of being alive? Whether I could explain it or not, at that defining moment, I knew I was indeed alive and part of the world; I was a *being*. For the first time, I became aware that I was a person. I was free, able to explore, and I knew that I existed.

That moment has stayed with me throughout my life. I was not frightened by it, even at the time; instead, I was elated. It was a beautiful way of connecting to the world.

When I was twelve years old and sitting alone with my grandfather, he suffered a cerebral hemorrhage and died. I was the last person to see him before his death. Only recently have I come to realize that the powerful *moment of being* I experienced in the garden, while chasing the butterfly, is connected to my grandfather's love. That memory of knowing I existed has made me feel very much alive, just as my grandfather did. As a result, I've lived a life of exploration, traveling all over the world and loving that I have the freedom to do so. I have lived exactly where and how I wanted. My grandfather's presence and my lifelong devotion to him have been a central part of my state of being. He is very much alive in me.

A-A-A: Map the Moment

What was the moment of *Awareness*?

_____

_____

_____

_____

What was the moment of *Acknowledgment*?

_____

_____

_____

_____

What was the *Action* taken?

_____

_____

_____

_____

Analysis of Moments
Dr. Debi Warner, Clinical Psychologist

Most of us feel that we are zipping along well in life if things go as planned and our road is smooth. When we are in our groove, we assure ourselves that all is well, and tell ourselves that we are "on track." We tend to value the predictable so much that we may be overwhelmed or worried when our plans go askew, or when unusual things happen.

Moments of Being... Finding Your One Moment in Time reveals that doors can actually open for us with these unusual events, creating experiences which can fulfill our dreams and fill our lives with deeper meaning—if only we recognize these events when they come. Like jumping onto a moving train, if we don't grab hold, these *moments* will slip past, and we will never see what great horizons might have been in our future. So will you know when such a moment has come? Will you use it to reshape your approach to life and advance beyond yesterday's horizons?

Many of us would love to have full control over our plans and lives, but our greatest human features may be our abilities to adapt and grow. Biologists define the ultimate human characteristic as adaptability. We learn through stories and lessons: it is through such understanding that we can apply life's opportunities and make good of it.

Barrie Brett has brought together special stories of love and triumph, inspiration, even sadness, which show our human potential and our adaptive spirit when facing these unpredictable and fleeting moments in time. Reading these stories, one can be assured that such events are opportunities to change our lives for the better. It becomes clear that our lives are more than we each can see, and that our recognitions and reactions to momentary opportunity and adversity are transcendent, and bring us to our ultimate worth.

Holding these stories in your mind, being touched by the ways that vulnerable ordinary people have captured and realized their own essence while facing uncertainty and even catastrophe, you can be reassured that facing the unpredictable can be an opportunity to realize your own future. So take a breath, reach for your higher meaning, grab it, use it, and have courage. It is in such *moments of being* that we are most truly human.

Moments of Being: Map Your Moment

If you were given directions to a friend's home, you might expect to follow a map with street names, avenues and landmarks to help you find your desired location. In creating awareness of something less concrete—like a moment that may have, or already has, changed your life—you will find it helpful to use a similar tool. Using the steps outlined in this chapter, you can literally map your own experiences to help you find your way to your desired future. Will you be ready to take advantage of opportunities that come your way?

In researching this book for almost fifteen years, interviewing hundreds of people, and attempting to understand the value and mysterious quality of moments, I have asked myself a series of questions. The answers have been enlightening, but they all come back to *Awareness, Acknowledgment* and *Action*!

Moments of Being: One Man's Experience

Before you begin mapping your own moment, it's important to understand that not everyone experiences a moment as transforming as those I've related throughout this book. In fact there are some people who go through what others might consider life-changing moments, but although moved by the experience, they do not necessarily feel changed. Sometimes the awareness and acknowledgment of these moments come much later and may be revealed in a subtle way.

Here's an example:

Ed Jacobson is a successful television executive. After graduating from high school, he was in a serious car accident that threw him out of the car and into a tree, collapsed his lungs, broke his ribs and shattered his arm. Doctors didn't believe he would live. When Ed did recover, he felt unchanged. "Yes, I did feel fortunate to have survived," he says, "but there was little difference in my life, except that I had to start my first year of college a semester late."

Years later, Ed experienced another moment that might have changed someone else's life: he won the Maryland Lottery. "I had purchased a number of tickets, but I didn't watch the drawing on television that night. The next morning, I opened the newspaper and placed my tickets in front of me. I slowly peeled off the numbers on each ticket like I was playing poker. Then, one ticket became much more interesting. All of the numbers matched: I'd just won the lottery! My heart started pounding so hard I thought it would pop out of my chest. But after collecting my winnings, I didn't feel changed. I just looked at that moment as another fortunate incident, another stroke of good luck."

There is one moment though that he feels did alter his life. "Several years after my car accident, I saw a movie called *The Hanging Tree*.[8] In the film, there was one scene that affected me deeply and began to change the way I looked at life. One line in particular really resonated with me. It said: 'To really live you must almost die.'

"At the time, I didn't feel changed by my accident and near death experience; I knew I had come close to dying, but I didn't dwell on that fact. But at the moment I heard the words in the movie; I began to see things differently, and to acknowledge the good luck I have experienced in my life. I had never really described myself as a lucky person. Today, I do. I survived a car accident, and I won the Lottery. Not many people are ever so lucky in their lifetimes."

It took a while, but Ed did develop an awareness about his moments, and was able to acknowledge their impact on his life. The action for shaping his future and applying this new understanding is up to him.

Moments of Being: A Few Suggestions

Understanding—perception, attitude, awareness, or whatever you choose to call it—can totally change how you look at a moment. It's my belief that the *awareness* and *acknowledgment* of what's happening at any given moment can alter how you look at your life and how you feel about yourself, and that the *action* you take can make all the difference. Everyone in this book faced pivotal moments, but because each person followed the three A's, they changed their lives.

If you found yourself in their shoes, how do you think you would react? Would you choose to go into the Peace Corps, or start a graduate degree? When hearing a doctor's diagnosis of potential heart failure, would you fall apart and give yourself up for lost—or would you do something about it and begin an exercise regime? If you found a wallet with thousands of dollars in it, would you keep it—or would you return it to the owner and stay true to your word?

I hope the mapping activities that follow will open doors to your future and help reveal choices for how you lead your life. If you find that it's difficult at first to map your own moment; you can go back into the book, select some of the stories, and imagine how each outcome might have been different had the subject taken a different action. If mapping a recent moment is painful for you right now, you might want to look back on your life and map something that happened years ago, something that you're proud of or that you wish had turned out differently. Without judgment, try mapping to see if the action you took might have brought about a different result. Also, if you're a history buff, you might find it easier to start by mapping historic moments that changed the direction of life as we know it.

However you ease into this process, the goal of mapping your moment or moments is to bring you one step closer to creating the life you want.

Moments of Being: Your Moment Revealed
The blank Map in this section is your tool to help you recognize the experiences which shape who you are and who you can become. Throughout this book, I've talked about the three A's; *Awareness, Acknowledgment* and *Action*. Now is the time to try and incorporate these thoughts into your own experience and see where it might lead you.

To get your map going, let's start with a few basic questions about your day.

- Did anything unusual happen?

- Did you meet anyone who stands out for any reason at all?

- Did you hear or see something that has stayed with you the whole day?

There's no need to over-think it: just take your pen and paper or turn on your computer, and start mapping your moment in the chart that follows. After seeing your observations in black and white, you may be pleasantly surprised as to how much clarity this gives you in understanding your life and its direction.

You might be aware that something unusual happened today, but have not yet been able to acknowledge its significance. Or perhaps, you do acknowledge that something unusual happened today (or in the past), but you're not ready to take any action. No problem. The important factor is that you are beginning to have *awareness*.

Following is a Map for you to use as you chart your own path. As an example, I've mapped out my own moment, so you can see the process at work.

Moments of Being: A Challenging Moment (an example)

The moment I've mapped for you brought significant change to my life, as you'll probably remember from my introduction to this book. Examining my moment through this mapping process helped me gain clarity, and helped me to realize that my moment of change, while painful and negative, also brought about many positive outcomes.

Mapping My Moment
Did anything unusual happen today?

Although I've never liked taking any form of medication, I ingested a health food supplement I was told would help with my lack of sleep.

Was there a direct result?
The product turned out to be tainted, basically poisoning me. After being hospitalized with unusual life-threatening symptoms, I struggled to regain my health. In the process of being so ill and not being able to work, I lost my income, my business, my car, and my life savings.

What can I gain from recognizing my moment?
I gained the knowledge that I could survive a most challenging medical crisis, suffer many losses and start over.

A-A-A: Mapping My Moment

What was the moment of *Awareness*?

(What is my moment?)

*One day I was a healthy young woman. After ingesting a tainted
health food supplement, my life and health changed completely.*

What was the moment of *Acknowledgment*?

(What has changed or shifted because of that moment?)

*I knew something was very wrong with my body and had to find a
way to get better.*

What was the *Action* taken?

(How can I best handle the situation?)

*Awareness and Acknowledgment were immediate but Action
took time. When I was a little stronger, I took steps to improve. I
sought help from a variety of doctors, researched magazines and
newspapers to find more information about my mysterious illness,
and finally moved away to re-launch my career and my life.*

Following is a map for you to chart your own path. I hope your journey will be a rewarding one.

Here are a few questions to help you start Mapping Your Moment.

Did anything unusual happen? (Today or in the past)

(Did I meet anyone who stands out for any reason at all? Did I hear or see something that has stayed with me the whole day?)

_____

_____

Was there a direct result?

_____

_____

What can I gain from recognizing my moment?

_____

_____

_____

A-A-A: Mapping Your Moment

What was the moment of *Awareness*?

(What is my Moment of Being?)

_____

_____

_____

What was the moment of *Acknowledgment*?

(What has changed or shifted because of that moment?)

_____

_____

_____

What was the *Action* taken?

(What Action could I or did I take? How can I best handle the situation?)

_____

_____

_____

Contact Information

Several of the people who shared their moments with us have meaningful books, CDs, and websites I believe you will enjoy. A few others have started charity organizations; I've included contact information below.

F. Murray Abraham	*A Midsummer Night's Dream: Actors on Shakespeare.* Series Editor: Colin Nicholson (Faber and Faber, Ltd. 2005)
Brendon Burchard	*Life's Golden Ticket* (HarperCollins, 2007) www.LifesGoldenTicket.com
Gary Hirshberg	*Stirring It Up: How To Make Money and Save The World* (Hyperion, 2008) Stonyfield Farm Entrepreneurship Institute At the Carsey Institute University of New Hampshire
Bob Kindred	For CDs (including Live at Café Loup): www.bobkindred.com
Marc Klionsky	*Marc Klionsky*, John Russell & Nicholas Fox Weber (Hudson Hills Press, 2004)

Jim MacLaren	The Choose Living Foundation: www.chooseliving.org
Sherri Mandell	*The Blessing of a Broken Heart* (Toby Press, 2003) The Koby Mandell Foundation: www.kobymandell.org
Liz Neumark	The Sylvia Center: www.thesylviacenter.org
Lynn Pierce	*Break Through to Success, 19 Keys To Mastering Every Area of Your Life* (Morgan James Publishing, 2007) www.LynnPierce.com
Valerie Smaldone	www.twosidesofacoin.com
Bonnie St. John	*Succeeding Sane, Making Room For Joy In a Crazy World* (Simon& Schuster, 1998) Other books include: *How Strong Women Pray* (Faithworks, 2008) www.bonniestjohn.com
Mark Strand	*Selected Poems*, Knopf, 1990 Other books include: *Blizzard of One* (Alfred A. Knopf, 1998, Pulitzer Prize Winner)

Dennis Walters	www.denniswalters.com
Dick Young	The Denan Project: www.thedenanproject.com
Micki Dahne	www.mickidahne.com
Dr. Debi Warner	www.renovationpsychology.com
Barrie Brett	I hope you will contact me and share your Moments of Being. www.barriebrett.com www.mymomentsofbeing.com

Credits/Endnotes

[1] Passage excerpted from *Moments of Being: A Collection of Autobiographical Writing* (2nd Edition) by Virginia Woolf; Edited by Jeanne Schulkind (A Harvest Book, Harcourt, Inc., 1985)

[2] Lyric, "525,000 moments so dear"; from "Seasons of Love," *Rent*; Jonathan Larson (1996)

[3] Lyric, "Got the dream but not the guts;" from "Some People," *Gypsy*; Jule Styne and Stephen Sondheim (1959)

[4] Quote attributed to Albert Einstein. *The New Quotable Einstein* (Princeton, 2005), p.296

[5] Selected passages throughout Sherri Mandell's story are taken (with her expressed permission) from her book, *The Blessings of a Broken Heart* (Toby Press, 2003)

[6] "We as a society should not be bothered by noise made by evil in this world, but rather enraged at the silence of the good." From *Testament of Hope: The Essentials Writings and Speeches of Martin Luther King, Jr.* (HarperRow 1986)

[7] Excerpt from "The Tunnel" by Mark Strand; *Selected Poems* (Knopf, 1990), used with the expressed permission of Mark Strand.

[8] *The Hanging Tree*, directed by Delmer Daves; Warner Bros., 1959.

Acknowledgments

This project has been a passion of mine for a long time, and along the way I have sought advice from many people. I'm so grateful to each and every person who stood by my side: my family and friends, publisher, editors, graphic artist, all the writing teachers I've worked with throughout the years, and everyone else who ever read my drafts and offered valuable input. Most of all, I'm thankful to the people who shared their personal moments with me, and now with you.

Since this book has been over a decade in the making, there are a great number of people to thank. I hope to publish more books in the future—and have more opportunities to show my appreciation—but please indulge me by reading some of the names that follow. Support comes dressed in many fashions, but each person listed here is important to me. The order is random. If for any reason, you feel that I have omitted your name, please accept my apologies, and blame it on my temperamental computer, which has a tendency to delete important information.

These are the people to whom I owe my sincere thanks and gratitude. They have offered advice, love and positive reinforcement.

My mother, who read almost every story before her untimely death and who continually reminded me how wonderful this project would be and encouraged me to keep going.

All of the truly amazing people who shared their moments of being, I believe that their honesty and openness will help many others acknowledge their own potentially life-changing moments. Thank you!

To David Hancock, CEO of Morgan James Publishing: thank you for leading me through the publishing process. To publisher Rick Frishman and MJ advocate, Margo Toulouse, thank you for helping me to make the transition from the world of television to the world of literature almost painless.

To Mark Victor Hansen, who held an all day MEGA Book Expo at The Javitts Center that I attended; your advice was helpful. And thank you for having David Hancock on your speaker's panel.

To Candita Clayton for introducing me to Bryna René—a superb editor whose professionalism and dedication to detail is reflected on every page—and to Marianna Zotos, a gifted graphic artist whose talent and precision captured the spirit of the book inside and out.

To my friend, avid reader Gerry Koval, who offered insightful edits early on.

To my attorney Si Reitknecht and his wife Muncie Reitknecht for friendship extraordinaire.To F. Murray Abraham for his meaningful Foreword and his commitment to this book project. To Dr. Debi Warner for her insight, Analysis of Moments and friendship. To Marc Klionsky for his generosity in allowing me to include his moving art images. To Mark Strand for allowing me to include lines from his masterful poetry.

To my true friend Connie (Cannon) Aaronson, and my cousins Ellen Kallins and Richard and Camille Bennett, for always being there. The same goes for Gina Rogak, Celia Englemeyer and Sally Barnett.

To Dad, Grandma, Aunt Lil, Uncle Sid, Gert and Irving Appel: though you are no longer with us, I miss you so, and think of you every day. I'm sure that you must be celebrating now that my book is published, probably playing a game of cards with Mom!

To Darren Mark for being Darren Mark, Tom Murphy for his ever-flowing ideas, and Kitty Oliver for her spiritual friendship.

To my friends in deed, Morry and Joan Alter, Joan Sherman, Suki Moscowitz, Florence and Arthur Barr, Arleen and Larry Blocksberg, Terry and Sandy Pinsky, Paula Greenwald, Peter Kennedy, John Lieser. Aunt Gwen, Jayne Bray, Loryn Ashlee, Kimmi Auerback, Micki Dahne, my cousins, David and Peggy Kern, L. C. Aaronson, Debbie and Andy Ellinghaus, Abby and David, Judi Ager, Maxine and Ted Agen, Bob and Sherri Erickson (you know why), Gloria Rosner, Bev and Joe Albert and Sissy Wagner. Melanie Donahoe and Henry Tenenbaum; I'm forever grateful to you both for making my introduction to TV so effortless.

To my new friends at Manhattan Center Studios and to all of my colleagues who worked with me throughout my thirty-year television career! To Charles Salzberg for his superior and much-appreciated writing advice, Marcella Landres for her proposal editing, Nancy Kelton for early revisions, and Evan Rhodes (a most talented writer and the smartest man I know). To Ric Cherwin (an eclectic and talented individual), Lenore Salazar, Eva Mihovich, Kathy Wein, Eleanor Haray, Bruce and Karen Yaffe, Anne Dacko, Mark Gorny, Bernadette Taraski, Geoffrey Pollock, Mark Seiden, Anne Marie, Joyce Walseleben, Omar Burschtin, Sondra, Fiona Druckenmiller, Frank Lipman, Andy Martinov, and Dr. Yamaguchi for his acupuncture/lifesaving skills.

To my Camp Lakota friends—American University cronies including Jane and David Green, Myrna Roberge, Frankie and Stuart Taylor, Madeline Stackman.

To Jerrold and Sandy Casway, Lynn Hammer, Beverly Greenfeig, Peter Cohn, Bob and Shelly Katzman, Edie Lutnick (a special human being), Barbara Ghamashi, and Ira, Rita and Steffi Shore.

My friends at Prudential Douglas Elliman, including Corinne Pulitzer, Nan Marelia, Steven James, Lea Governale, Dora Abril, Randi Lombard, Huge Williams-Noble, Sally Musikantow, Dean Heitler, Haley Rush (for the extra effort), and Michelle Licata.

To Sophia Nash (a wonderful romance novelist; I appreciated the advice), Jim and Kris Duffy, John Ransom Phillips, the talented Kim Burke, Brady and Bridget Rymer. Kevin Yoon, Maryann Karinch, Bob Silverstein, Niki Vettel, George Thomas. Anne Phillips, Amy Belkin, Pat Krupin Rubin, Irma Birnbaum, Esther Muller, Evelyn Gorman, Mimi Liebeskind, Stacey Sherman, Sydney Skybetter, Patricia Zohn, Robert Zohn, Barbara and Mark Goldfarb, Obie O'brien, Alvia and Richard, David Appleton, Naomi, and June, Harold, Brett and Heather German, Great-Grandma Estelle.

To Betsy Ehrenberg, Richard Raiser, Motti Levy for introducing me to Marc Klionsky, Orly Reitkopp for introducing me to Jim MacLaren, Helen Arden for introducing me to Al, Carole Hyatt for introducing me to Valerie Smaldone and Bonnie St. John, Jennifer Bergstrom at Simon and Schuster for the helpful words, Janet Switzer for appreciated advice, and Lyodd Jassin for legal expertise.

Carmelle Druchniak, Leah Poller, Jennifer Hippensteel, Barbara Herman, Jessica and Jane Weiner, Sandra Berube, Sandy Bernstein, Erec Lindberg, Lily Arporn Koval, Rona Roberts, Ralph Sloan, Jill Abramson, Leighann Ambrosi, Jane Dentinger, Matthew Fischel, Jamili Murray, Prima Stephani, Roberta Ruggerio and Lee Klein (both remarkable women), Mark and Maria Fringos for research assistance, Steve Meyers, Tiffany Loria, Jennifer Robbins, Randi

Schatz, Rose Polidoro, Nanette, Steven Bartek, Mark Kornspan, Gail Lee, Norma Perlman, Susan Malawer, and my book club friends.

To my closest family members: my brother and sister-in-law, Andrew and Patty Goldstein, my niece Lucy Rose Goldstein and nephew Max Francis Goldstein, my cousins Gary, Debbie and David Leight.

And, most importantly, to the heart and soul of my existence: my children, my daughter Dana J. Brett and my son Adam J. Brett; my daughter-in-law Beth Brett; and the darling of my life, my granddaughter, Ilianna. "I very love you!"

Bonus

To invite Barrie Brett to speak at your group, organization or book club meeting, please go to www.mymomentsofbeing.com.

To invite Barrie Brett to present her workshop, *Making Moments Count*, and speak to your company employees and management about improving client and customer service, please go to www.mymomentsofbeing.com.

Thank you.

About the Author

Barrie Brett is an Emmy Award-winning producer/writer. She has produced a variety of projects, from commercials and celebrity interviews to talk and magazine shows, news and PBS documentaries. As executive producer, she helped develop lifestyle programming ranging from relationship and parenting to gardening, exercise, design and cooking shows—including *The Main Ingredient with Bobby Flay, Rebecca's Garden, Way To Grow, Late Date with Sari* and *Living Better with Carrie Wiatt*. A former teacher, she has also produced educational shows and videos as well as corporate programs and courtesy training tapes.

Barrie has an ongoing fascination with the ability of moments to transform lives. One of her favorite moments is captured in this photo. Here she is with her granddaughter: they're going down the slide together for the first time.

Photo by Adam Brett

BUY A SHARE OF THE FUTURE IN YOUR COMMUNITY

These certificates make great holiday, graduation and birthday gifts that can be personalized with the recipient's name. The cost of one S.H.A.R.E. or one square foot is $54.17. The personalized certificate is suitable for framing and will state the number of shares purchased and the amount of each share, as well as the recipient's name. The home that you participate in "building" will last for many years and will continue to grow in value.

Here is a sample SHARE certificate:

HABITAT FOR HUMANITY

THIS CERTIFIES THAT
YOUR NAME HERE
HAS INVESTED IN A HOME FOR A DESERVING FAMILY

1985-2005
TWENTY YEARS OF BUILDING FUTURES IN OUR
COMMUNITY ONE HOME AT A TIME

1200 SQUARE FOOT HOUSE @ $65,000 = $54.17 PER SQUARE FOOT
This certificate represents a tax deductible donation. It has no cash value.

YES, I WOULD LIKE TO HELP!

I support the work that Habitat for Humanity does and I want to be part of the excitement! As a donor, I will receive periodic updates on your construction activities but, more importantly, I know my gift will help a family in our community realize the dream of homeownership. I would like to SHARE in your efforts against substandard housing in my community! (Please print below)

PLEASE SEND ME _____ SHARES at $54.17 EACH – $ $_____

In Honor Of: _____

Occasion: (Circle One)   HOLIDAY   BIRTHDAY   ANNIVERSARY

OTHER: _____

Address of Recipient: _____

Gift From: _____ *Donor Address:* _____

Donor Email: _____

I AM ENCLOSING A CHECK FOR $ $_____ PAYABLE TO HABITAT FOR HUMANITY **OR** PLEASE CHARGE MY VISA OR MASTERCARD *(CIRCLE ONE)*

Card Number _____ Expiration Date: _____

Name as it appears on Credit Card _____ Charge Amount $ _____

Signature _____

Billing Address _____

Telephone # Day _____ Eve _____

PLEASE NOTE: Your contribution is tax-deductible to the fullest extent allowed by law.
Habitat for Humanity • P.O. Box 1443 • Newport News, VA 23601 • 757-596-5553
www.HelpHabitatforHumanity.org

Printed in the United States
218540BV00001B/5/P

9 781600 376245